Karl

“Keep thy friend under thy own life’s key.”

— WILLIAM SHAKESPEARE
ALL’S WELL THAT ENDS WELL

PATRICK HOURCADE

Karl

No Regrets

Flammarion

Contents

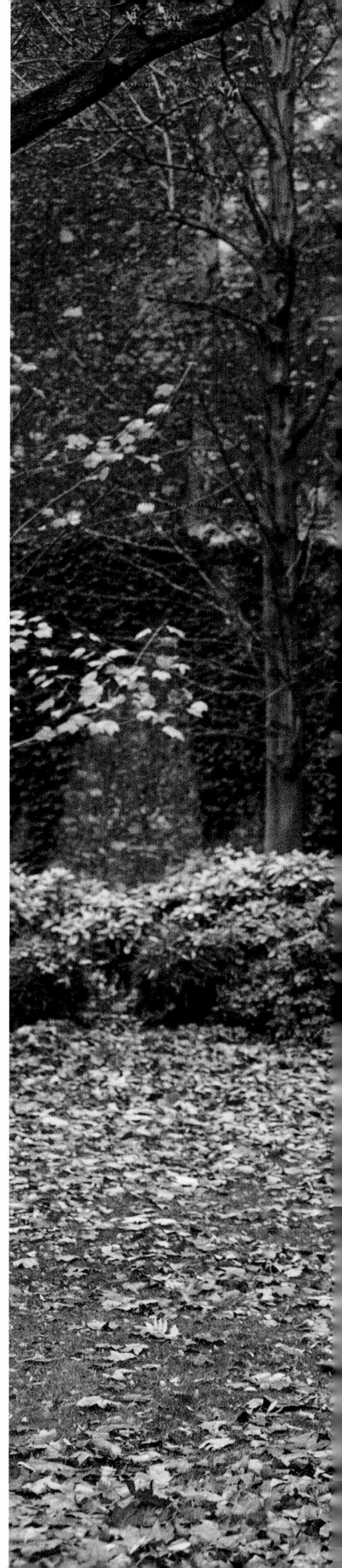

Herb Ritts accurately captures Karl's solitude and desire to remain aloof from things beyond his control. Here he is in the quiet garden of the Hôtel Pozzo, standing on a gilded wooden chair (a style he liked very much). His feet don't touch the ground, including the dried leaves, which he ignores.

After a show, I had to talk to him about his fashion. He was happy to and said, "Let's go home for lunch!"

 *and I*

"It was because he was he, and I was I."

How to write the inexplicable? The words of Michel de Montaigne, speaking of his friend Étienne de la Boétie, aptly sum up what others saw in our story without really understanding it.

Every time Karl bought a new house, he chose his room and wanted me to choose mine. Never, of course, did we share a bed. If we crossed paths in the morning, he was always very properly dressed, right down to his socks, wrapped in one of his famous white cotton piqué dressing gowns, grand hotel version, with the initials KL embroidered on the pocket.

In Paris, we each had our own homes, but I visited him every day in his studio to show him my discoveries and to watch him work, and in the evening I usually went to dine with him. I sometimes accompanied him on his travels; we always had some new and exciting idea in mind and the conversation never ran dry.

We were two loners, both rather reserved, the only indecency being our lavish spending.

We had a strange relationship, bizarre to others, not brotherly, not loverly, and especially not businesslike: we were accomplices. Of course we each cared about the other. There was a real attachment and a great deal of mutual respect, but our relationship was mainly a question of taste. Karl wrote to me in his last letter that we had been, both of us, very "naïve": this was the word he felt best defined us. In this he was right, because, thinking about it, we were like two curious children who loved only culture, who lived only for tomorrow, and quickly forgot the days gone by. We were two utopians, nonconformists in every way. We were two dreamers who loved to make our dreams come true. We were two lovers of an eighteenth-century art of living; not mimicking it, but inhabiting it.

We had the ideas and dreams to get ahead in life. He had the money I lacked, but that had no impact on our friendship. It was proof, if any was needed, that the most beautiful thing about friendship is complicity and sharing.

Time has passed, but before the veil of oblivion falls, I had to write this book.

"Knowing the past is one way to free yourself of it."

— RAYMOND ARON

Two friends, twenty-five years of complicity, twenty years of divorce. I write these lines, fragments of memory that resurface in my mind. They respond, revive, dialogue, and question one another, as they had always done in Karl's brain: "Order: it's when you accept your own disorder," he liked to say. It's up to each of us to find our own order.

No doubt Karl meant this as a gesture of friendship, but his sense of humor and provocation is clear. He knew perfectly well that this titillating photo was the opposite of me and would make me feel uncomfortable. He got his inspiration for the androgynous ephebe—all powdered up à la Barry Lyndon and sitting on a Jacob chair we had just bought—from a libertine novel by Louvet de Couvray. The story of the Chevalier de Faublas is occasionally funny, and ends badly, but is essentially about fidelity. This was our story.

Portrait imaginaire du Chevalier de Faublas

Pour Patrick
Joyeux Noël
et une heureuse
Nouvelle Année
et tendresse
Karl

KL. Paris 24.12.96

Grand-Champ, Château de Penhoët. In this vintage photo we still see the huge monkey puzzle tree on the right side of the mansion that we would soon remove. The Polaroid of Karl and me in front of our great project was taken by Jacques de Bascher.

Collage: Karl, Jacques de Bascher, and me; the house with its colorful furnishings; the painting of Voltaire and Frederick II.

I DO AS I PLEASE

He did not like conifers, firs, pines, or any resinous or spiny trees generally; he much preferred the leafy ones: "Pines, they go well in Italy, with Roman ruins and the blue sea." In front of the château in Brittany, there were two large trees. He called them "monkey trees" and he hated them, of course: "They are ugly and dreadful." I agreed with him. They made two large, unbecoming dark patches on the south side of the château. These two specimens of Auraucaria—commonly known as monkey puzzle trees because they are covered with sharp-edged leaves that make them very difficult to climb—were exceptional, according to botanists. Nearly a century old, they had grown to an imposing size and were, again according to conservation botanists, among the most remarkable on French soil. Karl didn't care, and their remarks only increased his distaste for those "monkey tails." He regarded them as enemies to be put down: "You agree that they have nothing to do with the classic image of an eighteenth-century French château." He had no taste for exoticism. So we ended up having the trees cut down. It was quite a scandal. The learned societies for the protection of Brittany heritage sent furious letters, which Karl hastened not to answer. He did not see any reason for such tearful complaints: "This is my house and I will do as I please. After all, they merely have to plant their monkey trees in front of Versailles."

Years later, he had the same reaction when he sold his enormous collection of eighteenth-century art, which we had amassed together over some twenty years. Among the masterpieces, there was a cycle of large tapestries of the biblical story of Esther, revisited in a Grand Siècle theatrical style. The cartoons for the tapestries are attributed to Jean François de Troy and now kept in the Louvre. "Our" very rare tapestries had conserved all their colors and were still in their original, sturdy, carved and gilded wooden frames. I had bought them for Karl, years earlier, at a memorable auction in Monaco of property from the Château de La Roche-Guyon. As soon as the gavel had come down, Bernard Tapie rushed to Karl and proposed buying one "under the table," implying that Karl would not have enough space to install the entire cycle. Karl, both delighted and furious, rejected his offer and said to me, "Of course we have enough room!" I placed them in the stairwell of Karl's first apartment in the wing of the Hôtel Pozzo in Paris, and later in the even larger stairwell in the center of the hôtel itself. Our plan was to put them in the grand salon in Grand-Champ, in Brittany, that was to be the highlight of the château, a home first and foremost, and eventually a foundation, dedicated to the Age of Enlightenment. But time had passed, the family members had disappeared, money was running out, and Karl decided to sell everything. The Ministry of Cultural Affairs had its eye on the tapestries. And, of course, there were some concerned curators, and even more thoughtful friends, who urged him to donate this prized cycle to the State. Karl kept telling me: "I should give them away, but why? I'm not even French. And if they continue to annoy me, I will do as I please and make pillows out of them!"

There were other monsters he had to deal with in Brittany. In front of the windows of the château, four large overgrown yew trees, ancient pachyderms, blocked the view and provided shelter to all sorts of creatures, including the bats that populated them at night. The misshapen trees reached just to the windows of the second floor, and completely blocked the view from the ground floor. The small garden, vaguely reminiscent of a French-style parterre, was disfigured by these somber former topiaries. I had them trimmed but Karl still thought they were too big, and their fate was soon settled. At that point the flowerbeds had to be redesigned.

I have never been good at drawing. Karl never stopped drawing, and paper and pencils were never lacking in his house. I immersed myself safely in the bible of French-style gardens, the drawings of Le Nôtre, and drew my version of a garden divided into four parts framing a small central pool. But my efforts to transfer onto paper what I pictured in my mind seemed pointless and doomed to failure. Karl wanted to see what I was proposing. I apologized for my clumsiness but he immediately replied, "What you mean is very clear and that's what counts in drawing." Those words encouraged me in all my subsequent graphic endeavors. Karl supported me in all my adventures, even the craziest ones. The thing he scolded me about most was that I didn't know how to shave. And in spite of all the razors I bought, no shave of mine ever earned a compliment from him. Jacques was always impeccable; I was more bohemian.

⁂

ANNA AND SAINT-SULPICE

It was Anna Piaggi who introduced me to Karl. I don't remember where or how I met Anna.

It was summer; no doubt there was a group of extravagant Americans, colorfully made-up, always on the move, never ceasing to pose, indoors and out, as if at any instant they might end up in some magazine. As for me, fresh out of my architectural history studies—very select studies that had aroused a passion and a vision of myself as a university researcher—I was not expecting any twist of fate. Corey Tippin, Donna Jordan, Pat Cleveland, Jane Forth, and Jay Johnson worked with Paul Morrissey for Andy Warhol. That day, they had caused a small revolution in me, an evolutionary leap. There I was, the tweedy professor, and they were super Pop: we were mutually exotic and have been inseparable ever since. It was through them that I met Guy Bourdin, Helmut Newton, and Anna Piaggi. At the time I knew nothing of the world of fashion.

Anna was stunning and radiant. Her voice, with her subtle Italian accent, was soft and agreeable, while her Cartesian intelligence was vividly contrasted with her unique, unimaginable way of dressing. Colors, forms, objects, baubles, accessories of all types, she mixed them all. She found an unexpected use for everything, for every moment, as only she could. Vidal Sassoon, the famous hairstylist of 1960s Swinging London, the creator of the geometrical bob, had cut her hair very short, neck-length, and put a streak above her eye, rigorously outlined in black, that meandered across her left cheek. Journalist, fashion designer, and columnist, she worked as she pleased for Italian *Vogue*, and was the muse for many fashion designers, who all loved her. The ladies of American *Vogue* were envious of her success and wanted to convert her to woman manager "basic" dressing—austere beige all year round. She responded, "I can dress 'basic,' too ... I go into my dressing room, turn off the light, and get dressed!" American women could never understand Anna.

One day she asked me to accompany her to Brasserie Lipp, "We've been invited by Karl Lagerfeld!" Then, in a sweetly babbling stream of words, she added, "You'll see, he's an extraordinary creature, remarkably intelligent, and very witty." She did not stint on praise; I absolutely had to meet him. She told me that he was always late, but it had already taken us so long to get ready that we ended up having to rush. At the brasserie I discovered a well-built man with a pale complexion, black hair and matching beard framing a square face, a monocle wedged under his eyebrow, and a collar that seemed to hold his head all by itself. He ordered a *salade de cervelas* and talked a lot, especially about a "château" that he had fallen in love with and just bought. He said it was nothing like an everyday Breton manor house—for him it was a miracle. "Imagine," he said, "a private Parisian townhouse, like those on Rue de Varenne, at the end of a sublime allée lost in the heart of Brittany." I listened to him attentively and ventured to tell him that it was possible, before he moved into his new abode, to purchase all sorts of period treatises on eighteenth-century houses. At the time, I was simply reciting my lessons on the subject. He looked at me in wonder, "Ah, very good, but do such things exist?"

"Yes sir, there are general treatises but also specialized ones on things such as carpentry, plumbing, painting, and much more."

"And you could find these books for me?"

This was the one and only time we addressed each other with the formal *vous* form. I rushed to the booksellers, to Drouot, and brought back works by Blondel and Dezallier d'Argenville on houses and gardens, works I knew by heart but that were new to Karl. His enthusiasm was immense. He waited for me in his apartment on Place Saint-Sulpice. "You know," he said, now using the familiar *tu* form, "it was Servandoni, the architect of the façade of the church that we have opposite us, who designed this house."

His apartment was on the corner with Rue des Canettes. The high ceilings made it very nice and airy, with décor out of a 1930s film. He continued in boundless delight, "I had some fun here, I made an art deco plan, but now I want to go on to something else." He was discovering the books I had brought him and learning quickly.

He invited me to the back of the house, where his mother Elisabeth lived a very quiet life. She looked like her son, with silvery-gray hair framing a squarish face. She had mischievous eyes and a very benevolent smile. "You are helping Karl with the château, very good." He did not miss the chance to show me a small painting by Menzel of Voltaire and Frederick II seated at a table with a circle of friends. It was definitely not a masterpiece, but as a child he had thrown a tantrum one Christmas to get his parents to buy it for him, quite clearly illustrating his visceral attachment to the century of Madame Pompadour.

The most impressive part was the heart of the house, a spacious room with modernist metal furniture, a wall filled from floor to ceiling with books, and utility tables, a drafting table (of course), and other tables covered with sketches—"my work" as he liked to call them. It was a beehive of beauties and talents of all sorts, constantly abuzz. Antonio Lopez was there with his friend and attentive advisor Juan Ramos, as were the stars of Warhol's Factory, the ones who had kidnapped me from my career as an art historian. They went on posing and took turns being sketched. Antonio took Karl's place and drew masterfully: his line was sharp, soaring, and dynamic. Karl drew with a broader, much less nervous line. There was a feeling of competition, where no one would be declared the winner. Karl said that he would have loved to draw like Antonio, but a sketch by Karl sent these young people into raptures, inspiring unrestrained compliments. I quickly understood that the key to all these activities was clothing. And here, Karl had his hand firmly on the tiller. He had just created over-sized silk shirts to be worn double over pants—the over-chemise was the new fashion. He added wide scarves in double-faced silk, which were also worn in pairs. We were well wrapped. I was part of the bunch and soon found myself dressed like the rest. Karl always treated me a little differently, he did not sketch me because he knew I did not like to pose. But here, everyone was trying to out-pose each other; it was a dandy contest, and when Anna came by with her extreme inventiveness and artfulness in creating the most audacious outfits, she was queen of the place.

But Jacques was special, I saw him as a brother right from the start.

⁂

JACQUES, THE BRETON

Fine-featured, with the eternal air of a dandy from another century, Jacques had a role model, a fictional hero he cherished from the bottom of his soul: Robert de Saint-Loup, Proust's ideal friend. A hint of a smile and a clear and sparkling eye complemented by a slender figure and inborn elegance, and always well disposed toward me: this was Jacques de Bascher. I never saw him make an inappropriate or vulgar gesture. He had a pleasing voice, always ready to laugh, and wordplay was one of his favorite sports. He and Karl never got enough of malapropisms, anagrams, spoonerisms, and other word games. In this he was an ideal partner for Karl. The Americans, of course, grasped nothing of these subtle feats of the French language. Jacques read English as well as he did German and had a good literary and cultural background. He wanted to be noble and more, and had vainly attempted to lengthen his name, stringing it on a long chain of particles: Jacques "de Bascher" was not enough, he had to add "de Beaumarchais." At that point Karl said to him, "Too many particles will suffocate you." Jacques was a royalist Breton in mind and spirit, he loved Brittany and the Chouannerie. But as regards France, Karl, other than Paris, knew only Saint-Tropez, and that only under a summer sun. One day Jacques organized a trip for Karl to discover his Celtic forebears. This was shortly before I met Karl. North of Vannes, in the Morbihan countryside, behind a small village, hidden at the end of a small valley, there was a nearly abandoned château that was up for sale. During the Revolution, Cadoudal, leader of the Chouans, had fought a battle there and one wing had been burned. Karl and Jacques were not able to enter that day and had to content themselves with peering through the gate. However, Jacques found a visual break in the garden wall, what architects call a "ha-ha," a barrier that doesn't block the view. Thus, through the tall trees, Karl could see the wing and the profile of the building. They also discovered a green maze in the park. Karl was swept away, madly in love with Jacques and madly in love with the château.

Jacques understood very quickly that I could help Karl restore this abode. He and I were similar personalities, the independent animal type, secretive and sensitive, often dreaming deep in our shells, aesthetes first and foremost but loving life and people most of all. We were animated by the same passion, to make Grand-Champ a unique place and a magical world.

Jacques didn't say anything about the cut trees. Karl and I had made the decision to restore the original spirit of the château. He had the utmost confidence in us as far as the house was concerned. I collected many documents on parks and gardens, and started hunting for woodwork and furniture appropriate to the décor that had existed at the time of the Revolution. Jacques encouraged me and congratulated me on my finds. But he wasn't always with us; he often took off to visit his family, or so he said. His family lived further south, in the Vendée, in the Château de La Berrière, a wine estate, producer of muscadet, of which Karl made abundant provision, and I had plenty of tastings. I later learned that Jacques was actually going to visit "his friends."

Karl did not like "Jacques's friends."

⁂

GRAND-CHAMP I

I have little memory of my first visit to Grand-Champ. I do remember that we arrived after a long train journey and then a taxi ride from Vannes station. A winding road hidden behind the village church led to the château. After a bend to the left and a turn to the right, the road began to descend and then opened majestically. As it passed through a small woods, a cathedral of old-growth trees formed a regal path leading into the estate. Further on, the trees gave way to fields lined with apple trees before closing in again and accompanying us all the way to the château.

The main gate was flanked on the left by a small chapel and on the right by some service buildings, all in the same style, from the Bourbon Restoration period. But what particularly delighted us was the very Pompadourian façade of the château. The Penhoët manor must have been rustic for many years before a marquis of Blévin acquired a position in the court of Louis XV, married the daughter of a shipowner who had become wealthy in the spice trade, and transformed the house into an elegant château in the style of the day. He even had stones from the Loire valley brought in to decorate the horseshoe-shaped dormers. His coat of arms in the center of the pediment was torn off during the Revolution, but the date of the completion of this metamorphosis, 1756, is still engraved in the stone. Karl never liked the name "Penhoët," which he translated as "wooden head" (i.e. blockhead), whereas in the Breton dialect it meant "woods' edge." He much preferred the name Grand-Champ (big field), which he believed translated to Lagerfeld in Swedish, although the actual translation would be *lang fält*.

As soon as we arrived, we rushed to our rooms: he to the large suite at the front on the left, Jacques in the attic above Elisabeth's apartments, and me in a small wing at the back. After Karl's mother discovered the place, she never wanted to leave it again. She took all her meals in her apartments. Old Marie, who had known the previous owner, a Monsieur Kraf, awaited us for supper, invariably with the vegetable tureen filled with sautéed new potatoes with parsley that we soon came to love.

The house was not refined. Of course the broad staircase with its balusters looked good, but it was made of wood, not marble or even stone. The well-proportioned windows were closed with the help of boards that I later replaced with steel and bronze espagnolettes. The ground floor had suffered a great deal before the last war, being inhabited by two penniless old ladies, who had ripped out the parquet floor of a salon for heat and so they could plant potatoes.

But earlier, after the Revolution, the château had been sold and enjoyed a second period of glory during the Restoration. Gates were installed and the chapel, guardhouse, and new stables were built. The gardens were certainly redesigned then and adorned with statues that can still be seen in old photos.

The days went by and Old Marie tried to impress upon us how kind the previous master had been. He had given her a large and dreadful painting as a gift. It was a nude and had a hole right in the middle. Marie refused to acknowledge the incongruity of such a sensual icon belonging to a deeply religious Breton. Karl hastened to point out that in German this type of painting is called a "Schinken" (ham), which was quite appropriate for the masterpiece in question. But he also offered to buy it from her, paying such a handsome sum for the eyesore that she could not refuse. He added that her would-be benefactor, obviously a womanizer, had blown his fortune gambling and sold off all the tenant farms on the estate before liquidating the house and what remained of the property. It was his wife who, at the turn of the twentieth century, had planted large black firs everywhere, and probably also the famous monkey puzzle trees that Karl so detested. She died young, of boredom, according to Karl, who continued weaving his tale, with dear Marie once a mistress of our pleasure-seeking, high-rolling gambler, the "gift" being the proof. However, looking at Marie, tired and worn out, it was hard to imagine such a storyline.

In the morning, she would bring me a big bowl of chocolate framed by two long baguette halves slathered in very Breton butter. In the meantime Karl had his tea—he didn't like coffee—and spent a good part of the morning dressing. When he was ready, we climbed into the car, often a taxi, for an outing. But soon, with Jacques—the best of chauffeurs—we went off cocooned in a vintage Rolls-Royce. The destination was always the same—Vannes, the old town where Karl had found quite a fine grocer's. There, an affable woman with delectable cheeks, a prefect's hairdo, and colorful makeup, wrapped in an immaculate white apron, proffered the most delectable of products. Karl was mad about the little cherry tomatoes but always waited for her cue, which was always forthcoming after each item, asking in her syrupy voice: "So with this, what else can I serve you?" Karl was enchanted and would repeat to us on the way home "*Alors? Avec cela, je vous sers quoi?*" That was all it took to send us back home laden with boxes of Pont-Aven's famous Traou Mad cookies, or the unforgettable local cake, the kouign-amann, an outrageous monument to the glory of butter and sugar, which capped off our every meal. But Karl could also not help crunching on a few Breton lace crepes, his guilty pleasure.

At that point, a nap was in order. Afterward, Karl did not want to begin working without first taking a stroll in his beloved park, which stretched along the edges of the estate on three main parallel paths. Karl had named each one of them. The one hugging the enclosure wall was "le Mail" (the mall), a name he had found in descriptions of the gardens of Le Nôtre. The "jeu de mail" was a game played with balls and mallets, a precursor of golf, pall-mall, and croquet, requiring a long court, or mall. The broadest path was simply dubbed "la Royale," while the third, running along the stream flowing across the estate, was "la Solitaire," even though he was never alone there. It led us on an enjoyable winding course back home. The hornbeam maze on the other side of the house demanded a great deal of care. Karl was very fond of it, although he never got lost in it; he was too cautious and detested the unexpected. "I hate surprises," he often said. "Good or bad!"

In the house, the ground floor had to be rescued quickly from damp. A contractor of questionable competence had doubled all the walls and plastered over everything. White dominated and there was very little furniture because the inhabitants spent most of their time upstairs on the piano nobile. There the old woodwork was soaked in a gray stain that made Karl quip, "The Goncourts were persuaded that this was Trianon gray when it was nothing but dirt!"

The walls still bore the wall coverings from the Restoration period. Yellow sun on burnished silk for Karl; Elisabeth had a blue Jouy canvas with the endlessly repeating motif of two women lifting sheaves of wheat. "These ladies tire me," she told me one day. "Tell them to lower their arms." In my room the canvas wall covering was red. I had large red and gold lacquered panels made in Paris in a distinctively French style. They came out well and Anna did not miss the chance to pose in front of them. The carpets on the natural wood parquet were worn, with holes in places. The décor was outdated, but it had known life, and we were quite happy. The first piece of furniture I found was very simple, with Louis XV lines, curves and counter-curves, but all finished in white lacquer, like fresh cream. Karl adored this style, and the matching cream. He quickly bought cans of fresh, rich cream, covering the Plougastel strawberries he ate so greedily. As for the red, there was some in the furniture, a table and two Italian chairs, which Anna used frequently when she posed for Karl, who was very excited to play the artist. At that time, the house was more like the Auberge du Cheval Blanc than Versailles.

We loved to laugh and talk about everything. Karl filled the rooms with the music of Strauss: *Elektra*, *The Woman without a Shadow*, and the inevitable *Rosenkavalier*. From time to time Mahler's *Das Lied von der Erde* took center stage. There was never a television in the château.

⁂

THE BEARD

He did not like his nose; he thought it was too big.

He would push his fingers up under his chin, telling me, "I hate old sagging chins, you are lucky, you and Jacques, you do not have that problem." I told him he was not there yet and that the way he articulated every word, his jaw thrust forward, would keep it from ever happening. But he asked me, "Do you think I should have a neck lift one day?" I answered, "Don't even start, you'll never finish!" It must be said that he had just shaved for the first time in a long while. His beard is a whole story in itself. We were in Grand-Champ. I think we were seeing the first hints of biological autumn, a few white hairs that dared to intrude on his beautiful brown beard. Of course no one noticed but him, but it was enough to make him resolve to give the coup de grâce to this bearded-Kaiser-with-monocle look. If Jacques's hero, Von Stroheim in Jean Renoir's *Grand Illusion*, was bald, Karl chose to go for a wholly different Nordic version, avoiding any Prussian allusion, even claiming that there were lots of brown-haired men in Sweden. No one dared contradict him on this ethnological point. Certain sharp, indelicate, and ill-intentioned tongues had uttered the opprobrious term "Kraut" in reference to our friend. At that time Karl wanted more to be Swedish than German.

But he had to go through with it: out came the razor. He did not warn us beforehand, and it was only the next day that he finally declared to me through his closed bedroom door, "I can't show myself, I wanted to shave, and I made a mess of it." Jacques was still sleeping. Lunch was still a few hours off. Karl ended up ordering breakfast and we left it on a tray in front of his door. I told him that time would heal everything and that he should use talcum powder in the meantime, like for babies. He had plenty of it and I imagined a moody Pierrot stomping about his room. When Jacques got up, I informed him of the developments, and we were very curious to see the result. He knocked on the

> ***"I hate old sagging chins, you are lucky, you and Jacques, you do not have that problem."***

door. Karl refused to open it, telling us that he had hurt himself, that he had cut himself several times. I concluded that he had used a good old cut-throat razor, like they used to do in the military in the last century. Jacques and I choked back our laughter and redoubled our good intentions, telling him that he was among friends, no one would see him, Marie would say nothing, and he had to come down to lunch.

The waiting began. It took a good hour, at the table, drinking wine and gorging on fine charcuterie that was well beyond being an appetizer, before we finally discovered Karl's new face. He was still wearing his dressing gown, like a suffering patient: the most astonishing thing was his head, which seemed to have doubled in volume. The talcum powder did something to hide the color, but not the rest. We tried to reassure him, "It's nothing, it's normal, it will pass..." Marie pretended not to see anything, only mentioning to Monsieur the next day that he looked better that way.

After the pain had passed, Karl, insatiable champion of work, began searching for a new look that would be more compatible with his now beardless image. Black glasses made their definitive appearance, especially because they hid the first wrinkles and a look that he found "too maudlin, like a lovesick puppy." As for his chin, the iconic fan would take care of that complex for many years to come.

⁂

Eija Vehka Aho, the icon; Juan Ramos, artistic director; and Jacques, the dandy.

The two talents: Karl, a bit jealous, and Antonio Lopez, king of illustrators.

Karl exhibited his first photographs in a small gallery on Rue Bonaparte. Anna Piaggi chose to dress soberly. We had just returned from New York, where we had been working for Vogue Italia.

Dunand, Printz, Ruhlmann, Follot—Karl's room on Place Saint-Sulpice was a hymn to art deco. He had also found this Jeanne Lanvin coat with step-pattern gold-embroidered sleeves.

Guy Bourdin found the perfect studio in Karl's apartment. He made me play ghost for Vogue.

Karl always loved the world of paper: books, magazines, newspapers, stationery, notebooks, notepads, Sennelier drawing pads. During his art deco period, he still kept things tidy. In this photo, Horst P. Horst deliberately left the Lalique glass, still with a little Coca-Cola in it, sitting on a pile of books.

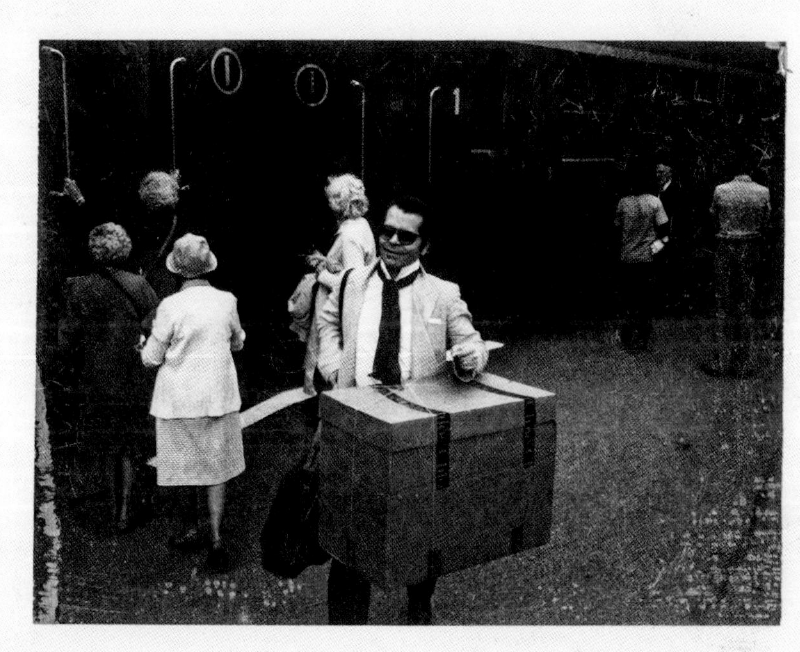

Jacques displays his character, complete with a very Boni de Castellane cane, through the lens of Philippe Heurtault. It was Jacques, the Breton, that drew Karl to the château near Vannes.

At Vannes station, Guy Bourdin plays paparazzo, getting a shot of our hero carrying a trunk.

Anna Piaggi loved Secessionist Vienna, Poiret, Art Deco, Futurism, but she especially loved posing.

AH, BEAUTIFUL DAYS!

Grand-Champ was in an uproar. Jacques and Karl were very upset: a film director whom both found terrible was directing an advertisement for Karl's new perfume Chloé. I had helped Karl conceive of the stopper, with its two Lalique-style calla lilies, for the round bottle. I had also created large anthurium brooches in the same style for the last Chloé show. Karl took the art deco aesthetic as the guide for this project. His favorite film, *L'Inhumaine* by Marcel L'Herbier, with set design by Fernand Léger and Robert Mallet-Stevens, was the source of all his inspiration.

So there we were, immersed in Louis XV décor, when we saw the vintage Rolls arrive. Jacques was ready and already attacking the director, seeking to convince him of his latest idea, to turn the Rolls around, and he was right about that. Karl, as usual, kept us waiting. He prepared with all the meticulousness of David Suchet playing Hercule Poirot and was likely to be a while. We bided our time, waiting around the small round pool in front of the château for the star. Peacock pigeons, the only guests allowed in the park at the time, graceful birds with virginal white plumage, fluttered here and there. It was a beautiful day. Jacques had calmed down and asked to have his makeup touched up. At that point, seeking to assert his importance, the director began asking loudly, "What is the use of this little plank of wood at the end of the pool? Was there some ingenious system for draining the water?" Suddenly there was a loud crash as the two shutters on Elisabeth's salon window flew open. The silver-haired Madame poked out her head and angrily addressed the would-be scientist: "The board helps fish go for a walk in the park!" She immediately closed the window and went back to listening to her Beethoven. We had a good laugh. I eventually told the troublemaker that the board was there to allow the pigeons to drink from the pool.

Anna came to Grand-Champ only three times. Karl did not especially like her Australian lover, Vern Lambert, a redhead with a brawler's physique. But Vern was very kind and attentive to his beloved, for whom he had left his vintage clothing boutique in London. Anna had been his favorite customer and he now devoted his life to her. He had good knowledge of fashion history but Karl wanted to make it clear who was superior in this field. Taking care not to upset him, Vern played the part of a simple courtier.

When Anna knocked on Karl's door in the morning, she had already spent a good hour choosing her clothing and look, and Vern could go back to bed. One day she arrived wearing a black apron over her pants, the next day a Poiret evening gown, but the ritual was always the same. Karl waited for his muse, exclaiming each time: "I have to draw you!" That was all she was waiting for. In the meantime, I was in the next room redesigning the château. I liked this room very much, a nice square space, with two windows giving onto the forecourt and one on the side. Karl had let me move in, and I had gladly given up my room at the back to Anna, who needed more room for her clothes.

The few pieces we had of Louis XV furniture, in the colorful, provincial style of this first phase of redecorating, served as the backdrop for Karl's illustrations, down to the small wallpaper screen on which Anna rested her hand. Anna, patient and delighted, could pose for hours, but was then very impatient to see the result. Karl loved to sketch Anna; drawings of his muse were everywhere in his room. He took real pleasure in bending over his sketches, surrounded by an armory of colored pencils and felt-tips, sometimes working in watercolor, which he found quite challenging. After lunch, Jacques took us to Erdeven, where we managed to find a secluded spot on the long beach far from the local bathers. Once, when Karl came with us, we put a chair and small table in the trunk so he could draw. Anna, always on the hunt for accessories, found some seaweed that she displayed like scarves from the sea. The evening aperitif was muscadet from La Berrière and a variety of sandwiches. I flipped Jacques's surfboard over and set it with crystal glasses and Meissen plates, against a background of sand and the pink sky of the setting sun. It was worthy of Fellini.

Jacques could not stay long in one place and often left us alone in the château. In the afternoons, I liked to visit Elisabeth. She never came downstairs but asked me a lot of questions about what was going on down there. I told her about local happenings and she told me what was happening internationally. She read newspapers in both German and French and kept me well informed. She was anxious for work to begin. I had promised I would redo her room as a first priority, replacing, of course, the old faded canvas on the crumbling walls with bright, sunny Chinese wallpaper with large flowering trees, inspired by mid-eighteenth-century decorations. When it was done, she was happier and more cheerful than ever. A few months later, Guy Bourdin would take a photo in this new interior.

Karl was not particularly fond of oriental art, and so he surprised us when he brought back three brightly colored mandarin coats embroidered in gold.

They had come from the collection of a Lady Kelly. They were collector's items that would be at home in a museum, but they ended up on our shoulders. Jacques had chosen the green one; Karl was undecided between red and blue, eventually choosing the former, leaving me with the blue. At the candlelit dinner, we looked like a Siamese delegation come to greet Louis XIV. The next day he wanted us to wear them again. He said it was the perfect outfit for Grand-Champ. One day, during the afternoon walk, while Jacques napped, we were outside the main gate and Karl wanted to venture a little further on. We were talking about the future of the château and had started along the path bordering the wall when a farmer appeared on his tractor. He greeted us and then said to Karl, "Ah! Monsieur Demis Roussos!" I looked at Karl. At the time he still had a full beard, no ponytail, his hair was loose down to his shoulders, all mantled in a fire-red Chinese coat. The reference to the Greek singer, who was quite popular at the time, was quite fitting. The funny thing was that it was usually Karl to make such more or less flattering comparisons. We were in good spirits when we returned inside, but Karl never wore the oriental coat again.

Strolls were a daily ritual at Grand-Champ. We even took them on summer evenings, when things had cooled off and the moon lit up the park as if it were day. One night the spectacle was particularly prodigious, with thousands of fireflies lighting up the park and the surrounding fields. Another time we were at the edge of a meadow and a cow started to chase me. As I fled I heard Karl's voice behind me, "Ah, behold the fearful city-dweller! You see, I know cows from my father's factories." He was referring to his father Otto's condensed-milk factories. Having recovered from my impromptu bullfight, I asked him if he had been around cows much. He answered that he had seen a lot of them in his youth.

Jacques stayed in his room reading, drinking his beloved whisky, and smoking. We met at the table where he would tell us of his readings, especially the biographies he particularly liked. Karl had very quickly rejected Jacques's morbid fascination, as romantic as it was sadistic, with Louis II of Bavaria or Gilles de Rais. Jacques had just read the memoirs of Lou Andreas-Salomé, friend to Nietzsche and Rilke. Karl was not to be outdone on this subject and suggested a few other historical figures, "Have a look also at Nathalie Barney. I am not too crazy about feminists, but she is special. Not like these poor girls nowadays who are always attacking men. They are tiresome and always end up as lonely, greasy-haired spinsters."

⁂

FRANCINE

Women were a big part of Karl's life, not only for his constantly reworked visions of fashion and style, but also for their presence, their intuition, their infinite ways of being, and their capacity to help, to stimulate and enliven the explorations of his work, his projects, and his simple everyday life. He wanted to be a loner—none of them could replace his mother—but he needed their attention and liked their company. Some women left a more significant mark on him than others. These women shared a particular trait, essential for dialoguing with him: intelligence.

When Karl started to work for Chloé, Francine Crescent had been named fashion editor at *Vogue Paris*. One summer day in Rome, I ran into her on the Spanish Steps and she talked me into coming to work with her. Francine is irresistible and our adventure together lasted more than fifteen years. This tall blonde was the very image of modern elegance; there was no other female player in the fashion world who had her look. A slight smile, no makeup—or just a touch—a prominent nose and broad forehead, the blonde hair of a Nordic girl, and a clear icy gaze that made you melt. She always dressed in a very sober navy blue suit and white T-shirt. Sitting in the front row at fashion shows, she had her own way of crossing her long legs and straightening up to hug the big spiral notebook that served as her computer. Impeccable. A discerning mix of frigidity and seduction—she drove men crazy. Fellini, Hitchcock, and many others sought to seduce her. She loved them all, without desiring them, and featured them in her magazine, which she made unique in those years. Bourdin, her favorite photographer, was one of these men. One day, he was on a beach in Normandy sketching the buttocks of a woman. He was very sheepish when she suddenly turned around and it was Francine!

Karl adored Francine. She lived in an atelier on Rue Raynouard that had once belonged to Edwige Feuillère. Karl created a light gray sofa for her, very designer, and broad white drapes with art deco trimmings. Years later, the day that Condé Nast, after removing her from *Vogue*, in turn fired me, he avenged us by pulling all his ads from the magazine. It wasn't really a proper thing to do, but it was his way of telling us that he loved us.

Francine came to Grand-Champ. I was delighted and left her my room. Karl let me use the room next to his. Francine loved the simple life: wine, seafood, literature, and cinema, and going to have her morning coffee at the bistro on the corner. We took her to the sea with Jacques. She loved being in the sea, swimming, and laughing. Karl never sketched her. Unlike Anna, Francine was not big on dresses and the history of clothing. She hated posing and only liked people who could make her laugh. Karl was perfect in this role. She had loved the château in its early "campground" state and wanted Guy to come to do a series of photos.

⁂

GUY BOURDIN

Francine adored her stay at Grand-Champ and called Guy as soon as she was back at her magazine. "Patrick has an idea for you; you are going to be invited by Karl Lagerfeld to his château in Brittany." Guy liked Karl very much, amused by his extravagant luxury, his endless inventiveness, and especially his fascinating culture. On the train back from Vannes, Francine asked me to come up with an idea so that Guy could shoot some photos at the château. I suggested a doll theme. The clothing we had seen at the last show would be perfect for it. When I told Guy about my idea, his only response was: "Can we break one?"

It was spring, the camellias were in bloom, and the first roses had begun to brighten the garden. The weather was fine; everything was going as well as it could. Karl worked in his room and the troupe was bustling about on the ground floor. Guy had brought his son Samuel, still a child. Naked as nature intended, Samuel ran with the girls around an apple tree. The girls were Audrey, a strawberry blonde, something that appealed greatly to our artist; and Nicole, the master's faithful dark-haired model, who had a very strong character. I immediately brought a sofa out of the château; we put it under a tree and Audrey passed out on it. We were making images that were very sensual but also very romantic. Guy could not help casting Nicole as the martyr, he fantasized seeing drops of blood beading on her breast. After all, we were in Brittany, land of Calvary, and *Vogue* was used to Guy. Nicole also played the broken doll, fallen from the balcony onto the stoop. Guy loved it and wanted to do another series with other girls. He came back to Grand-Champ. He was having a great time and everything was going well. Then one rainy day—it did rain from time to time in that paradise—Guy imagined a shot with a fireplace. The fireplace was made of blue-gray stone, a work of pure Louis XV style quite befitting the château. It was in an empty white room, which would later be

"Stop everything! You'll burn down the château! My mother is suffocating, you're smoking her out!"

paneled and become a library, something Karl greatly needed in all his houses. A girl dressed in chaste white was positioned in profile on a chair in front of the fireplace. A fire was lit. It looked like it was coming right out of the girl's sex, which is exactly what Guy wanted. Everything was perfect and ready to go when Karl burst into the room shouting: "Stop everything! You'll burn down the château! My mother is suffocating, you're smoking her out!" It turned out that the chimney was blocked at the roof and all the smoke had flowed back into Madame Lagerfeld's apartment, which was just above. Karl was already phobic about fire—he refused to let anyone burn logs in the fireplaces—and now, even worse, we had given his mother quite a fright. It was the only time Karl ever lit into me, but I must admit I deserved it. I went upstairs to apologize to Elisabeth, who was still in shock. That evening, however, the conversation went off blithely in a completely different direction and Karl was again in a good mood. Francine liked the photo very much. Nothing was ever normal with Guy.

⁂

SAD EPISODE

One day, Jacques introduced to Karl a sad but affable young man who wanted to do business with him. He was supposedly one of Jacques's "cousins," as was the tradition in Brittany. José started to work and to follow Karl to Paris and New York. I did not fully understand his role or function, but he was always there, at Grand-Champ as well, a familiar face at the château. There was no bedroom for him there so he lodged in a small hotel not far away. One day while I was having a bath, he burst in and launched into a declaration of love for me. It was detestable and I told him to get out immediately. He persisted and I ended up getting angry. Karl wasn't there so I told Jacques about the embarrassing situation. The following day, when Francine and I were on the train about to leave for Paris, José appeared on the platform to say goodbye. He had the droopy air of a scolded dog. Francine noted that and said to me, "That young man looks quite sad." Our train left. I never imagined what would come next. Some time later, I was at the château with Karl, as we were getting ready to go down to lunch. A car arrived and we heard loud voices on the ground floor. I could not see who they were but they were demanding that I come down right away. Jacques came in at that point and told me to stay with Karl. He went down in my place and spoke to the arrivals, who eventually left. When he came up he looked at me with a sort of smile but his face was pale, "José has just committed suicide. He left a note blaming you. That was his family." I was appalled—horrified and revolted at the same time. I insisted that I had never given José the slightest encouragement. Karl intervened. "Patrick, you have nothing to blame yourself for. You had nothing to do with it, if José killed himself it is because he was an embezzler who was about to get caught." Jacques confirmed Karl's allegation and told me that he had informed the family of the real reason for the poor boy's death.

Jacques was more of a devil than José, but he had rescued me from an ugly mess. He was much more courageous than Karl, who in this case proved to be more a manipulator than a savior. This sad event brought Jacques and me closer together; I saw him as a brother, although we did not share the same destiny.

⁂

1970s PARIS

Before he had his own cars and chauffeurs, Karl used to spend all day in taxis. He never stopped crisscrossing the city, between the right and left banks. He had thousands of things to do but still took the time to go to the cinema with us. He, Francine, Jacques, and I regularly piled into a cab in the evening like perfect cinephiles. Karl was our mentor; he usually chose the films from among the latest releases but also many off the beaten track. One of them in particular, Éric Rohmer's *The Marquise of O*, made a strong impression on us for its lighting effects and intimate, timeless atmosphere. The lighting had been designed by a master, Néstor Almendros. Karl, Jacques, and I had been enthralled by the power and mystery of his use of candlelight in this film. From that point on, we made sure our dinners were lit by this magical source. We also went to theaters dedicated to the incunabula of cinema to rediscover the early masterpieces of the seventh art. The fare ranged from Tarkovsky's *Mirror* to Fritz Lang's *Metropolis*. After that we would go out for dinner: caviar on the Champs-Élysées, mussels and fries in Montparnasse. Routine and exoticism were the two main ingredients in our evenings. Karl was particularly fond of a restaurant on Rue des Beaux Arts called La Route Mandarine. The honey-roasted spare ribs were his favorite for their sweet-salty flavor. He washed them down with Coke, we with muscadet. But during the day, the office-salon was and will always be Café de Flore in Saint-Germain. The menu those days was very frugal, but that did not bother Karl, who ate only frankfurters, while he read a pile of newspapers from the nearby newsstand. Another necessary stop in the neighborhood was the bookstore La Hune, which was next door at the time. There the ritual was always the same: browse downstairs in a counterclockwise direction, then up the small spiral staircase for more browsing upstairs. We came out of there loaded with packages of books, most of them for him, but a few for us as well, according to our tastes—which he wanted to develop, of course. But we were not yet finished with our provisioning. Across the street, on the corner of the boulevard, next to the Brasserie Lipp, there was the Drugstore. It was a quirky, golden place that drew us in as if by magic—you could find anything. Cigarettes and whisky for Jacques, cosmetics for Karl, a cream for this, a cream for that. "You should try it," he said to me, pointing out his favorite kind of Kleenex, the biggest ones, XXL, in the red and black box, which he bought in great numbers. It was now time to go home and drop everything off.

Karl adored Paris. "I wanted to come to this city ever since I was a child. My mother used to get the *Figaro* fashion album in Hamburg; everything in it was fascinating to me. Nothing was going on where we were, in the provinces. Paris was a magic lantern, it was where I wanted to be." Now and then he would tell us about his first arrival in the capital, coming out of the Gare de l'Est and discovering Rue de Maubeuge by taxi. "I was horrified by the dirtiness," he confided. "The walls were all gray. Malraux had not yet cleaned up the city. But once we got to the Latin Quarter, the atmosphere was completely different. And then I discovered the Champollion." The "Champo" was the quintessential art-house cinema, a historical monument annexed to the Sorbonne. "It was there that I really learned French. I often sat through the same film several times in a row, listening carefully to every word, or reading them scrupulously when there were subtitles." It is true that Karl had no difficulty with the French language. He had an excellent and broad vocabulary because he had read the classics, but was also quite familiar with the language spoken on the street, even the slang of old "Paname." He spoke in fast bursts. "Do you think I have an accent?" He fretted somewhat about that. Everyone else said he had an undeniable German accent, no doubt sustaining their "Kaiserly" view of him. Strangely enough, I didn't find that Karl had an accent; I certainly had a friendlier ear and was quite simply more accustomed to it. But I never heard him sing.

In addition to the collections, which he never stopped developing, one after another, he also had time in those days to spend evenings at Le Sept, an exclusive high-end restaurant with an irresistible nightclub. On the ground floor, with a discreet entrance off Rue Sainte-Anne, the décor was bright with large mirrors, a bit of greenery, and lots of white tablecloths. Jacques had brought his muscadet from La Berrière so we did not need to consult the wine list. Francine did not come here, but Anna and Florentine were often at the table with us. Florentine Pabst was without doubt Karl's most loyal female friend for close to half a century. She, too, was from Hamburg. Her beauty had made her a heartbreaker among rock legends, Jim Morrison in particular. Unlike other muses, she remained reserved, mysterious, but always also delightful and charming. Karl asked to be her son's godfather. She had named him Karl out of fascination for a man she considered a star from the start. He was a rising star at Chloé at the time, she was a journalist among journalists. But for forty years they never stopped talking, she in Hamburg, he in Paris or elsewhere. Up to a few days before he died, Karl was sending her notes morning and evening.

After dinner we went downstairs into the cellar, all aluminum and mirrors, where the Cuban magician Guy Cuevas, star DJ, kept us dancing into the wee hours. We twisted this way and that, never stopping, to rhythm and blues, soul, disco, and a host of other musical cocktails and treats concocted by Guy. It was a starry night in that cellar; fashion came to life in creatures that wanted to be both oracle and creative spirit, whirling as if out of a dream in an imaginary movie. The trip was permanent and I personally did not need drugs. Dancing the whole night with Dona, Pat, or Loulou was enough to make me happy. I invariably ordered whisky and coke. I didn't particularly like it so it kept me from drinking; I didn't have time for that. Karl stayed clear of the dance floor. A real voyeur, he loved to watch the courting, the approaches, the escapes. Jacques did not dance much but flirted a lot. Kenzo loved to dance and did not hold back. His favorite partner was Loulou—Loulou de la Falaise, Yves's muse, inebriated, radiant, always laughing out loud, and always ready to faint at the end: her partner had to be there to catch her. Another one that Jacques was mad about and would eventually propose to was Diane. She was the daughter of Prince Marc de Beauvau-Craon and granddaughter of the multimillionaire Antenor Patiño. But beyond her pedigree, she had a natural madness that could not fail to captivate and bewitch our dear dandy. I liked to dance with Diane; she had gone so far as to shave her head. She laughed constantly and danced, or reeled, all night long. She had a precious cane, very Boni de Castellane, that she always kept with her. But it did not help her keep her balance; every dance with her was a dizzying experience. We were caught up in a whirlwind and came out exhausted, happy, and dripping, ready to do it all again the next day.

Le Sept was replaced by Le Palace; Rue Sainte-Anne sank into a murky, drug-induced stupor, lost its laughter, and became a death sentence for young men in search of love. The parties at Le Palace set the rhythm for Parisian life, breaking with the chic Rothschildian balls of the past. Jacques wanted to play the role of creator and producer; Karl encouraged and helped him. He made the curious choice of Venice as the theme for the place. Of course, Jacques had in mind the eighteenth century so dear to Karl, but he should have known that Karl hated Venice. Furthermore, and paradoxically, considering his choices of clothing and personalized cosmetics, Karl hated dressing up. I, too, traumatized by a Chinese costume malfunction during carnival when I was a kid, have always hated it. Karl said to me, "I'm like you, but we have to make an effort." His effort was a red silk evening coat trimmed with gold braid, explaining that he was not a *domino* but a *tabarro*, as he had seen in a painting by Pietro Longhi. Otherwise he never wore red. Anna arrived at the Hôtel Pozzo with a basket on her head filled to the brim with crustaceans. She explained that this was exactly what fishermen's wives on Burano wore in that period. Her costume was black and the animals were completely real and smelled foul. Karl begged her to get rid of them. She wouldn't listen to him so he refused to ride in the same car with her. Jacques, on the other hand, had to remove the Rialto Bridge from his head to get into the car. In her day, Marie-Antoinette had special carriages and coaches to accommodate her great scaffolded hairdos. As for myself, my trick to escape the masquerade was to pin a series of postcards from the city of the Doges to my jacket, front and back. I thus spent my evening as a sandwich-board. After that, nothing replaced Le Palace.

⁂

SEX AND SOCIAL LIFE

One, no sex; the other, too much...

In Karl's case, it doesn't make sense to speak of homosexuality because he had no sexuality. Not so for Jacques. One evening, Jacques gathered us for a private screening of a cerebral porn film, where a pale, blasé lady gave her body, without appetite or enjoyment, to equally pale, equally glum-looking men. The room was greenish, the skin was greenish, the woman was presumably in hell to suffer this bitter punishment. We left the room worn out and Karl summed up the evening by saying, "The idea was interesting but it was boring in the end." He and I had hated the film, while Jacques, of course, had found it thrilling. Irredeemable vice, unremitting punishment, eternal damnation—Jacques doubtless identified with this seedy character teetering on the edge of despair.

That Karl refused to have sex with his lover, ignoring whatever effects such abstinence might have on his own health, may seem perplexing. But it may explain Jacques's parallel life and his descent into a living hell. Jacques manipulated others coldly, with cynicism and irony. He had always done that. Faced with Karl's refusal to love him carnally, he ended up playing that venomous, perilous card.

Otherwise why would Jacques have seduced and then debased Yves Saint Laurent as he did? At the beginning of the story, it was Pierre—Pierre Bergé, the fashion designer's patron and official lover—who wanted to dominate Jacques the dandy, to drag him into bed with him. Pierre was very good at it. Jacques, clever and perverse, quickly understood that the weakest link was Yves. The bachelor pad at Le Dragon was the theater of a torrent of sex and laughter. Karl told me about the time that Jacques had sex with a boy while Yves was locked up in a cupboard to better suffer and enjoy at the same time. Karl was a voyeur, but from a distance. Pierre demanded they break it off, which did not faze Jacques at all, while Yves played the part of the spurned tragic heroine. Pierre had publicly heaped scorn on Jacques, but as soon as Jacques was out of the room where he had been with Yves, Yves pulled out a photo of his lover, pressed it to his breast, and said, "I adore him!" Karl rejoiced; Jacques loved only him. At any rate, the rivalry between the two designers is subject matter for another chapter to the story. Pierre got hurt the most, and even after Jacques was dead he was still raging against him. He claimed that Jacques had dragged Yves into drugs, as if he had needed any encouragement. Much later, after the death of Jacques, Pierre produced

"In life, there are no problems, there are only solutions."

a ridiculous, demeaning film with an uncouth gigolo who was supposed to represent Jacques. I was very shocked and sorry for Pierre, who could not get over his hatred toward him. He was still denigrating him on TV shortly before his own death. Pierre did not like failure, but great demons survive for a long time in the minds of the humiliated.

⁂

NARCISSE NOIR

Karl always spent a great deal of time in front of the mirror, but Ruhlmann's large round mirror was his favorite.

When I first met Karl, he had a full head of brown hair. I never saw a trace of what he called mahogany, a criticism his mother had made to him when he was a child. His full beard was just as brown. One day we found him with his hair tied back in a ponytail. He said that it was better that way, but he soon admitted that he was starting to lose hair on top—the monk's dome was showing through. Claude Montana had the same problem at the time. A woman who was an expert on the question examined their scalps and saved them both from disaster. She advocated stimulating blood flow to the scalp with special brushing, which only she, of course, could administer. But she also said they should not get their heads wet. To keep them clean, her solution was lycopod powder. So it was this strange dry shampoo that one day gave Karl's hair a new style that would remain for the rest of his life. The very dry powder increased the volume of the hair, which was pulled back in a ponytail: the state of his cranium was kept under wraps. A little later, when our friend's keratin began to whiten, her solution was even more radical: full white powder. At a time when he was saying he had turned the page on the eighteenth century, he was rediscovering the customs of the court of Louis XV.

"In life, there are no problems, there are only solutions," quoth Karlovich, as we sometimes liked to call him when in Jacques's company. Thus, for his supposedly short—or rather, average—stature, which had made him suffer so much when he played Hercules with Juan in Saint-Tropez under Antonio's lens, he quickly adopted high heels, in the style of Monsieur, brother of the Sun King. Over time, he found more suitable and fashionable tricks to cope with this complex. Even when he was in slippers, I never paid attention to his height.

His great love as regards the art of living and looking was perfume. Even before he was able to join the essences game with the great "noses" of the perfume industry, Karl was a perfect customer and connoisseur of the major names in scents. His favorite house was Caron. And among the many perfumes he collected, Narcisse Noir was unquestionably his favorite. But he liked all of them, Nuit de Noël or Tabac Blond, which was suitable for Jacques, the smoker. And when he finally had the opportunity to create some of his own scents, he never looked back.

Karl was scrupulously attentive to his appearance; it was a rule of life for him. I know other Narcissuses, who forget that you're even there, anxiously and furtively seeking reflected glimpses of their fleeting beauty at every opportunity. This was not our friend's case at all. Once he had completed his self-inspection in the mirror, out of sight of others, his drawn-back hair, well-powdered complexion, and black glasses—full screen and final protection for his eyes, at times tired from too much work—all shouted narcissism, when in fact all he was doing was obeying his own inflexible discipline: impeccability.

⁂

IMPECCABILITY

"You don't know how to shave," he said to me. I could hardly accuse him of the same: once he had lost the beard he was always clean shaven and the rest of his presentation followed suit. His shirt collar immaculate, rising high to accentuate the form of the head, the jacket, the vest when he wore one, without the slightest imperfection—a picture postcard of the chic, elegant man, a fashion icon out of old prints. He also added a tie pin, always precious and often original. He was the perfect representative of his genre. He never looked like anyone else, and always surprised everyone. They always found him original; he thought of himself as normal and the others ordinary.

Nothing repulsed him more than the banal and the ordinary. Jacques and Anna felt the same way and were devoted adepts of this religion. Not wanting to see me sink into vulgar costumes and customs, he insisted on sending me boxes of tailored shirts embroidered with my initials, with a collar slightly lower than his own. Hilditch was his favorite brand of shirts at the time and I regularly received large navy blue boxes with the "KL" label he had designed, usually containing white shirts, but sometimes striped. These were the only shirts he wore. And that's how I went to work at *Vogue Paris*, with, of course, the de rigueur tie pin. He and Jacques had their jackets and pants tailored to perfection at Cifonelli's in Rome: "You can spot a Cifonelli shoulder at twenty paces," he claimed, and he knew what he was talking about. For my own wardrobe, I went to Rue Nélaton in the fifteenth arrondissement in Paris. Karl had discovered an old-school tailor there, a real magician. A dimly lit, cluttered shop at the rear of the ground floor, its walls completely covered by hangers and dark suits, was the realm of Monsieur Poretta. He had a pale complexion, a languid gaze from under romantic brown bangs, and a timid smile. He took your measurements deftly, barely grazing you, then drew pins from the cushion on his wrist and adjusted your clothes without a single prick. In a voice with a hint of exoticism, a soft mix of Italy and the Balkans, he would tell you that you needed to come back for a second fitting. Prêt-à-porter? We were well into the realms of high tailoring. I would sometimes have to wait weeks before I could finally slip into an absolutely perfect suit.

Sometime earlier, I had discovered a passion for ice skating. Every evening I would go to the ice rink and turn, leap, and pirouette, with only modest skill because I rarely took lessons. The main thing was the speed and the music. I felt released after hours of that and went to bed deliciously tired, without stopping at the nightclub. Karl saw this as an excuse to design me a pair of pants with a high waistline. They gave me the look of a flamenco dancer, which I really liked. Karl also adapted an outfit for a skating champion, writing on it, "Skating: some do it, others roll it."[1] It was pure Karlovich! As for Monsieur Poretta, he ended up working for the fashion ateliers at Chanel.

For his travel needs, Karl turned to the Fendi sisters, whose grandfather had started out as a saddler. Their suitcases and bags became iconic thanks

1. *Rouler un patin*, "roll a skate," is slang for French kissing.

to Karl's famous stripe, inspired by the alternating light and dark woodwork of Vienna Secession furniture by Thonet. He did not remain entirely faithful, later buying luggage from Goyard. But the ritual was always the same: no fewer than four suitcases for a short trip. He never forgot to slip in a small pillow with a white (and later black) case: he liked to have a warm belly on the plane or train, and thus also avoided soiling his pretty clothes with the ink from magazines or newspapers.

⁂

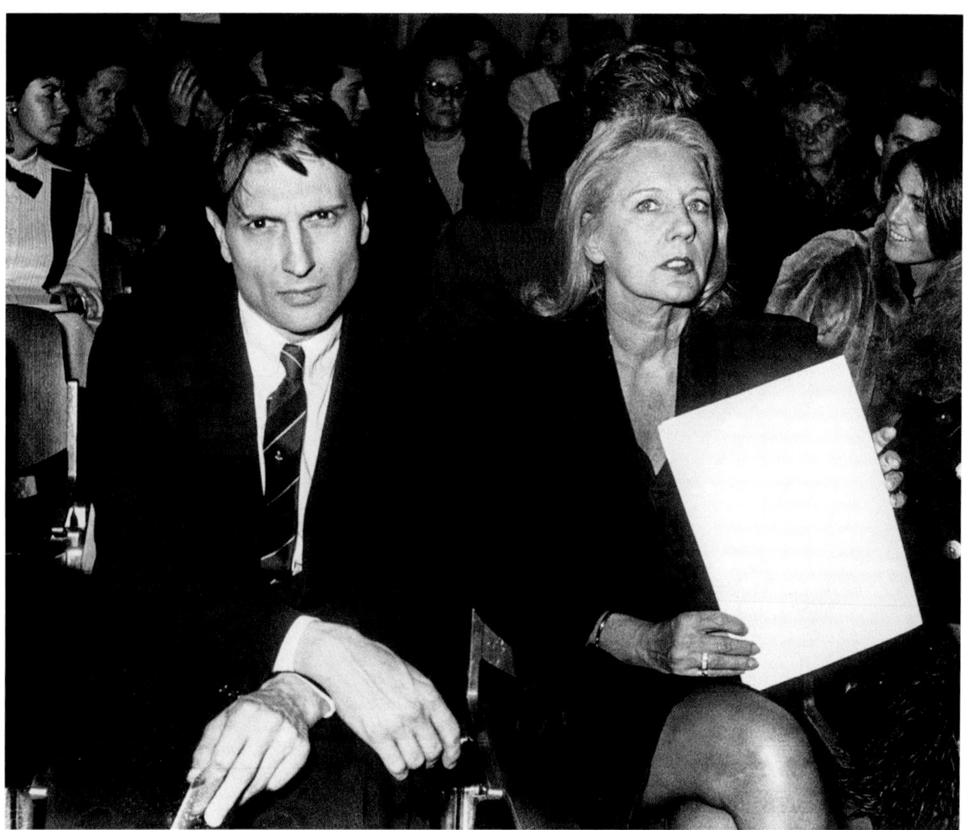

Francine Crescent changed my life, introducing me to the world of photographers: Bourdin, Newton, Horst, Lartigue, Bailey, Beaton, Sarah Moon, and many others she loved. While she thought fashion designers were geniuses, she saw photographers as gods. Karl adored her, Vogue *was her world, and I was part of it.*

Horst never started work without a Campari from the café next door. Over the years he worked in the United States and Europe, he gave fashion some of its most iconic images. Time had forgotten him, but Francine went looking for him, and he was proud and delighted.

Guy Bourdin was an enfant terrible. *When he loved you, you had to accept his conditions. That's how I ended up as a corpse floating in one of the château pools. Shoots with him were endless adventures—but Karl objected to the fire in the fireplace.*

Paris: parties, high society, the whirlwind of fleeting passions and vanities. Jacques de Bascher played cat and mouse with Pierre Bergé and Yves Saint Laurent. His Venetian Ball at Le Palace nightclub was a revolution in the art of nightlife. Karl was perfectly happy to play along.

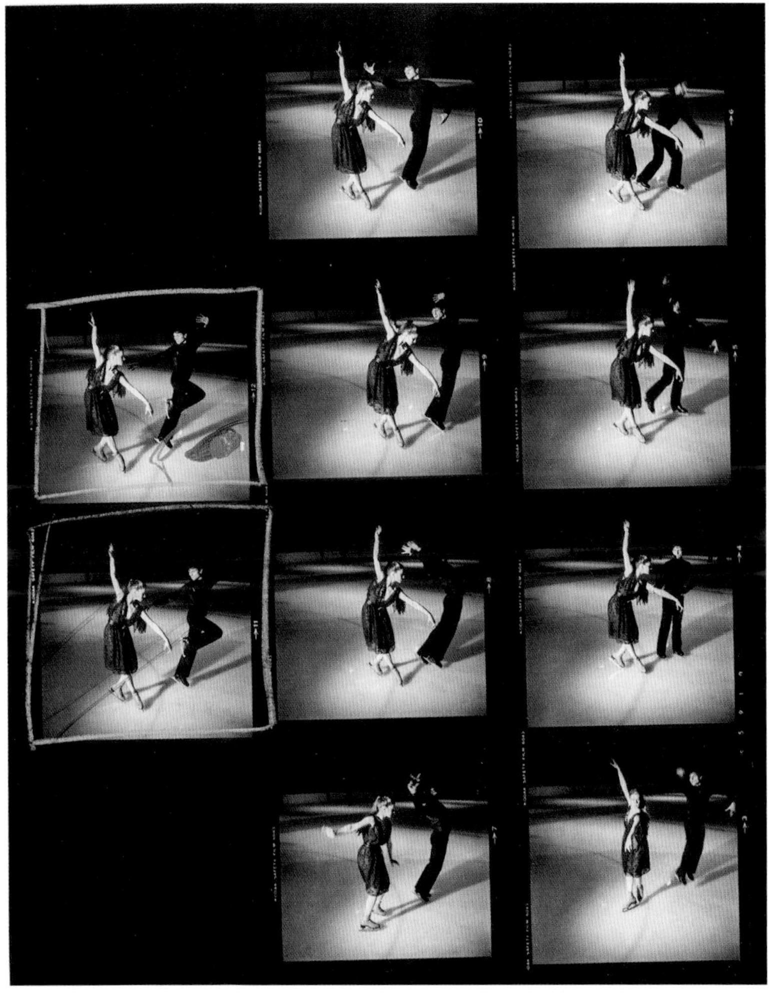

For Karl, posing was a discipline. His scarf is printed with one of his designs for Chloé. In addition to the high collar, his search for his famous look would soon include a monocle.

My favorite sport at the time was ice skating. Karl insisted on dressing me for it and Horst came to photograph me.

In this wing of the Hôtel Pozzo, the woodwork came from the Tuileries Palace, in front of which Birgit de Ganay poses on a Cresson chaise longue. The portrait of Bach that Karl had just purchased from the Stasi, the East German secret police, hangs over the mantelpiece behind him. The carpet features the coat of arms of Louis XV, while the large bronze between the windows was created by Falconet for Catherine the Great. This realm of luxury and culture, his everyday life at the time, was published in Paris Match.

An earlier photograph of the same room features different furniture and décor. Like for his own personal look, Karl strove for perfection in each part of the house. Change was part of his art of living.

MONTAIGNE

Moving day, furniture lined up along the wall, books piled on the floor, and it was only the beginning. We had only one aim: carefully follow the example of the Duke of Choiseul, whose snuffbox provided complete illustrations. To begin, we hung the paintings so they were almost touching, like in the duke's bed chamber.

Our inspiration: the snuffbox, painted by the miniaturist Van Blarenberghe, represents the bed chamber of the Duke of Choiseul in his mansion on Rue de Richelieu.

Bed mania: a collage of some of our beds. We had become true experts. Catherine the Great's four-poster is at the center left.

THE EARLY POZZO

When he left his apartment on Place Saint-Sulpice, Karl abandoned art deco. From then on he only wished to live in the atmosphere and spirit of the Age of Enlightenment: Louis XV and Madame Pompadour, Voltaire and Frederick II, the intelligence, culture, and opulent refinement of a world he saw as ideal. The curves, the luxury, comfort, and ergonomics—for him it was all there was to be said.

He inaugurated his new house in the Hôtel Pozzo di Borgo, Rue de l'Université, hosting a dinner for the wedding of Paloma Picasso and Rafael Lopez-Cambil. He called me the following day because he wanted to furnish it properly. We were an amazing duo: I, the former art historian, now the artistic director of *Vogue*; he, the increasingly fashionable and successful stylist, soon-to-be guru at Chanel. We shared the same passion, far from fashion and frippery, for the eighteenth-century art of living. I had built up a solid collection of old treatises on homes and gardens, and we bought all sorts of books on the subject, and about furniture, of course. While the first furniture we bought for Grand-Champ was modest and whimsical, in Paris the quality was incomparable. We had a predilection for chairs; Karl called them "morphologically benevolent with remarkable ingenuity and ergonomics." One style in particular attracted our attention, mixing the curves of Louis XV with the classical elements of Louis XVI, a transition style known by scholars as "à la grecque." We bought everything that seemed essential for building up an exemplary collection from renowned antique dealers and from auction houses.

The color, or rather the colors, were our main concern. A small-scale antique dealer in the Saint-Germain district, Monsieur Comoglio, clued us in on the secret of old wallpapers. He had materials that had kept their original colors since the eighteenth century, and he had them replicated faithfully. Far from the supposedly chic pastel tones that were fashionable among the bourgeoisie, we discovered bright and bold colors. A royal blue salon, golden yellow curtains in another room, the dining room with natural paneling enlivened by red windows, while green was perhaps the most appropriate color for the small study at the back. Liliane de Rothschild, who closely followed our adventures in style, had a snuffbox painted by Van Blarenberghe in the 1770s. It was decorated with miniatures of the most beautiful rooms in the houses of the Duke of Choiseul, and was an absolute reference in our case. Liliane gave us photos of this little masterpiece. Each room was an icon for us. Most of our friends kindly thought of us as kooks, until one of them, Alexandre Pradère, an expert in the field, challenged by our audacity, decided to study the colors of antique furnishings for himself and ended up proving us right. He even gave a conference on the subject at the Getty Museum. Not even Versailles could get the better of us. Later, when the collections were sold, a very influential lady in the high-chic fashion world said to me, in a tone that was meant to be imperious, "I saw Karl's art collection, I saw how he upholstered his chairs. What bad taste in his choice of garish colors!" I just smiled at her. She was wearing beige, of course, and was oblivious to the fact that I was also in on this bad taste.

Whenever I found an object, a sculpture, or a painting, my thought was never simply "this will please Karl." I knew what I was looking at and felt justified in each of my choices. We both loved the treasures that we were accumulating. Karl's financial means increased every year and our purchases followed that fortunate trend. At first, after having left the apartment on Place Saint-Sulpice to Jacques, who stayed there writing his sad biography of turpitude and vice, Karl lived in the apartments of the left wing of the courtyard of the Hôtel Pozzo. A grand marble staircase with wrought-iron bannister led up to the piano nobile, which had three large salons, a small study, and a bedroom giving onto the other courtyard. The walls were finished in white and gold, or a natural wood paneling known as "Capuchin" at the time, or with silk. A leading expert in furnishings, Bruno Pons, informed us that the sculpted cornice in the antechamber came from the Château de Bercy, which was destroyed in 1861, and other woodwork came from the Tuileries Palace. There were large, high windows everywhere and thick carpets on the floors. Karl, of course, would have preferred Versailles parquet, but he was intrigued by the soft, dark ocher layer that gave ever so softly and voluptuously under our feet. He was sure there must have been not one but two layers of carpet. Stylistically it was a blunder and to hide it we bought vintage French rugs, which gave us an even thicker cloud to walk on. A great lesson in Enlightenment decoration, following period paintings and drawings, the curtains were very simple: silk taffeta hung down to the floor from blackened iron rods. The light came through as if entering a cathedral through stained glass. But the rooms were never finished; our enthusiasm for new acquisitions kept leading us to change their identity. A salon became a ceremonial room, a dining room became a study, a study became a small living room. We were running out of space.

Daily life here was very lively. One Christmas day, Florentine arrived from Hamburg with her suitcases packed with traditional German Christmas tree ornaments, fine silver tinsel that wrapped the tree in scintillating light. Karl had not seen a Christmas tree in his house since he was a child; it was something exceptional.

We had a usual ritual in the evening if nothing else was planned: Karl and I met in the black-and-white kitchen, an exception to the prevailing style of the house. A plate of frankfurters, enough to fill us, sat on a small table—a Mackintosh remake—with a big pot of mustard next to them for dipping. I drank La Berrière muscadet; Karl put two ice cubes in the big Lalique balloon glass he loved so much and immersed them in Coca-Cola. We talked the whole evening, dismantling and reconstructing the world. The household staff was minimal at the beginning: a Spanish woman named Mercedes who had been his faithful housekeeper since Saint-Sulpice. As she grew older, she became more befuddled, leading to dangerous outcomes. She once cleaned Karl's teapot with bleach. He was furious, shouting that she had wanted to kill him, and fired her.

Fortunately, life had many other flavors. A self-proclaimed "Bavarian" brasserie had opened on the Champs-Élysées. Karl happily ordered Weisswürste, fine white veal sausages eaten with sweet mustard and warm potatoes with onions. The Munich tavern ambience was not to his liking, but the sausages made him forget the music.

⁂

IN PRAISE OF THE BED

My dear Karl,

It was pure madness, and in the realm of madness we found our rightful place. I helped you discover, through old drawings and engravings, the extravagant creativity of the Age of Enlightenment as regards the design of the bed. We were fascinated by the inventiveness and delirium of the era in creating monuments to the glory of Morpheus. We talked about it constantly and very often purchased exemplars. You were very happy to display your learning on the subject: French bed, duchess bed, Turkish bed, Polish bed, Roman bed, pulpit bed, or tombeau bed, the latter in the servants' quarters. Specialized vocabulary to describe the forms and types of beds found during the Age of Enlightenment; there was no detail we did not know. You loved to tell your guests that no fewer than a dozen artisans were needed to create these masterpieces: a carpenter, a wood carver, followed by a lacquerer or a gilder, or both, an upholsterer for the bedding, another for the stuffing, yet another to stitch the coverings, and one to apply the trimmings. Of course, the weaver was necessary for the silks and a trimmer to embellish it all with cords, various knots and rosettes, tassels and other indispensable accessories in the assembly of these grand playthings. And then the locksmith to install the wheels, handles, and pulls. And to crown it, the featherer, who planted a panache of plumes on top of it all. You did not fail to use the most appropriate vocabulary when talking about bed trimmings with experts: "pentes, bonnes grâces, cantonnières." *The scholars congratulated you and your guests were delighted, although they found it hard to believe that you could actually sleep there, when that is exactly what you did every night.*

We did so much we had to put some things in storage. Including the very beautifully embroidered bed where you posed in your Chinese robe, and which unfortunately disappeared when we moved. But many of these beasts already had their place at Grand-Champ.

The apotheosis was unquestionably the enormous Polish-style bed, custom made in France for Catherine the Great. It was intended, some say, for her palace in Tsarskoye Selo. The coverlet was damaged and richly deserving of restoration, but the cost was astronomical. It was silk embroidered "with partridges" after a design by Philippe de Lasalle, whom the empress had employed to finish an entire room in her palace. The bed was too large, and remained for quite a while at the bottom of the stairs.

It was later sold to the Getty Museum in Los Angeles, which unfortunately also gave up on the partridges because of the expense. As for me, my favorite bed was the iron bed, without plume or canopy. You had it in your room once in a moment of austerity.

⁂

TEA WITH RIFLE AT ELISABETH'S

At Grand-Champ, Marie had retired and a Spanish couple, Rafael and Pilar, had just arrived. He was brave, proud, and austere; she had dyed red hair that was frizzy from the hairdresser's habit of using small rollers, small laughing eyes, and teeth going in all directions. We could not understand a word she said. It might have been this language barrier that pleased Elisabeth, who very quickly became fond of the couple. She was like their mother and enjoyed their company, often summoning them for one reason or another. She had forgotten the horrible nurse at Place Saint-Sulpice, Monica, who was supposed to help her in her convalescence after suffering a mild stroke. Elisabeth never wore makeup and this dragon, this very *fatale* femme, in her nurse's costume of form-fitting white blouse and white cap, like in old Hollywood movie, would always take a tube of rouge from her pocket and spread it on Madame Lagerfeld's lips, saying to us, "She looks much better this way!"

Elisabeth was serene at Grand-Champ, far from rumors concerning her son, listening only to the radio and her beloved records. She was not one to move around much. Karl regularly scolded her for this lack of activity, "She refuses to walk, that can't be right." But Elisabeth did as she pleased, just like her son.

Rafael had one simple idea in his head for working at Monsieur's château, and that was to bowl him over. He found an amazing team of Turkish masons in Brittany who rebuilt the entire outer wall of the château. As for Pilar, she said that Monsieur was hardworking and that I was kind, but added things that were barely comprehensible—but clearly acerbic and nasty—regarding his friend Jacques, who was clearly not in the couple's good graces.

Meanwhile the immaculate white peacock pigeons gradually became stained by a large intruding wood pigeon. They now came in all colors and Karl could not stand seeing them anymore.

As for Elisabeth, she did not change, her large face remained wreathed in her close-cropped white hair. She was always well coiffed; she went to the hairdresser almost up to the day she died. She stayed in her room and I would visit her in the afternoon for tea. She didn't want the Biedermeier furniture that Karl kept telling us had come from the family house in Hamburg. Nor did she want photos of Otto Lagerfeld, Karl's father. Karl wisely kept these relics, including a small photo of which he was very proud, the port of Vladivostok taken by his father, who had worked in Russia at the turn of the previous century. Elisabeth, on the other hand, preferred music. The record player was always playing some well-known piece. No singing here, but a lot of violins and piano. Like her son, she was not particularly fond of Chopin, much preferring Beethoven. She often asked me to put on a record with a yellow label that read *Deutsche Grammophon – Ludwig van Beethoven – trio opus 11*. She wore a very sober loose crepe chemise that her son had once designed, always in a light, soft tone, mauve gray as I recall, over loose black Chinese-style pants. The only jewelry she liked to wear was a stalactite-cut rock crystal pendant surmounted by a coral bead. This precious and fragile object was hung on a simple black silk cord. Karl had given it to her when she arrived in Paris; it had been made by the jeweler Fouquet in the previous century.

Elisabeth often complimented me and encouraged me in the promising start of the château restoration. But she became more and more critical on the subject of Jacques. He smoked too much, he drank too much, he spent his time doing nothing. One day there was a small revolution. Rafael came to tell me that Madame wanted to see me. Pilar was standing in the room and Elisabeth was sitting on her sofa, both of them with their eyes glued to a shotgun lying on the small tea table. It was quite a surprising sight, completely incongruous in this room. Rafael told me that he had found it under Jacques's bed. Jacques's room was just above Elisabeth's. Their excitement had given way to great irritation. They were all talking together at the same time and I wondered why Rafael had gone to look under Jacques's bed in the first place. He thought Jacques wanted to kill him, startling Pilar into a bout of hiccups. Neither Jacques nor Karl were at home that day. Finally, Madame Lagerfeld said to Rafael, "Put it under my bed. He will not come looking for it here." Then she turned to me and asked, "What do you think? Should we tell Karl?" Personally, I was all for appeasement and peace in the home. But I was never able to convince Rafael that Jacques was basically a good person. Jacques later told me that he did, in fact, detest the two Spaniards, but the rifle was not there to kill them, but rather to clean up the interbreeding in the dovecote. That made more sense to me, but I could see that a page had been turned in the house. Karl acted as he always does in such cases, he turned a deaf ear: out of sight, out of mind.

⁂

For nothing in the world Jacques would have parted with his Hockney drawing, but he freely distributed Karl's drawings of him.

POMP AND DECADENCE

1980–1990

The new Grand-Champ was going to be sumptuous. I had lindens planted around the new pool, and we would also rebuild the wing that had burned during the Revolution.

The woodwork and beds arrived at the château. There were so many I had to keep an inventory.

Fashion correspondent and photographer Mary Russell captured Karl in an unguarded moment in his Paris apartment in the late 1960s.

THE REVOLUTION

On Sunday, May 10, 1981, France was running a fever, several degrees to the left, as the Socialists took power. Nobody knew what was going to happen. Would Soviet tanks roll into Paris? Would property be confiscated? Would the bourgeoisie be forced into exile? The results had just been announced on the 8 o'clock news: François Mitterrand had been elected President of the Republic. Francine and I were waiting at Montparnasse station for Karl, who was on the last train from Vannes. We were curious to see his reaction. We welcomed him with smiles but were not surprised by his reaction: he was devastated; he looked like he was going to a funeral. He saw it as a complete disaster for France. We assured him that it was nothing, that there were no Russian tanks in town, that Paris was as he had left it the day before. Our laughter finally won him over. As therapy for this terrible shock, he invited us to dinner at the Maison du Caviar, a symbolic choice given the country's shift to the left. It was only some time later that I understood what that date had meant for him. The new taxes were going to be a great existential threat for the moneyed. Switzerland and Monte Carlo were the havens for those who wanted to escape the new Socialist government's thirst for rich people's money.

One day, Karl told me that he was moving to a very modern apartment building on the seafront in Monte Carlo. It was called the Roccabella and was quite a piece of work. Of course, all we talked about was style and décor. I did not care that he was becoming a resident of Monaco and would thus escape nasty French taxes. But behind this decorative screen, another destiny was unfolding, one that would bring a complete change to his life, Jacques's life, and my life as well.

In Paris, once the initial emotions of the French Socialist revolution had subsided, Karl, now Monegasque, began to cozy up to the new regime, making overtures to some members of Mitterrand's government, starting with Jack Lang and his wife Monique. Karl laughingly repeated something Lang had said: "We are quite happy to be ministers." Reassured by these new relations, he remained intent on continuing all of his projects.

⁂

MONTE CARLO, MONACO

"Rainier is an intelligent man," Karl liked to say about the sovereign prince. He had adroitly maneuvered with respect to successive French governments and given his tiny state unexpected authority. Karl implied that he was close to the prince and that he had invited him to his famous fortress, but the person who would have the greatest and most enduring appeal for him in this new adventure on the Riviera was Princess Caroline. She was an exceptional person, combining congeniality and respectability in an entirely natural way. He said of her, "I adore Caroline, she is beautiful, cultivated, intelligent, and very funny, too. But you have to remember your place with her. If she wants dresses, I'll gladly make them for her, but she can wear whatever she wants." This remark was not insignificant because, at the time, following her mother's example, Princess Caroline was loyal to Marc Bohan, who did the collections for Dior. In any case, "glad rags" were not the focus of their conversation: she and Karl both loved French, English, and German literature. Karl liked to say that she was as cultivated as he was. At dinner one evening after Corneille's *L'Illusion Comique* at the Théâtre de l'Odéon, Caroline and he tried to outdo one another with literary quotations. They both had phenomenal memories; neither one got a word wrong. Years later, at his funeral, visibly moved, the princess would read a poem by Catherine Pozzi, Karl's favorite French female poet in his later years.

Another enchanting trait was her joie de vivre. As Karl described it, "She loved being the mother of a family *all'italiana*, surrounded by kids and cooking pasta for them." I have a very nice memory of when we were furnishing La Vigie. It was a house we had lusted after from the balcony of the Roccabella and we were at last converting it. That means we were spending all our time rearranging the furniture, day and night—Sundays, too—in what Karl called "fittings." That day we had decided to move a massive gilded wood console with a marble top to a landing. It weighed a ton but we were the only ones there to do it. But then, in the nick of time, the princess arrived and immediately jumped in to give us "a helping hand." Her muscles were indeed helpful.

But Monaco was more than that: there was Monte Carlo with its charities, parties, and many and varied ceremonies. Karl, as a proper subject, did not want to shirk his obligations as a good resident and followed princely etiquette. And so I finally had the chance to see him dance, not a common thing. He preferred close couple dances. He danced with a smile on his face, could not help making conversation, never stepped on his partner's toes, and kept in time. He had known how to waltz since his youth in Hamburg.

There was no shortage of occasions for laughter on the Rock. One day a wealthy lady was thanking an Italian princess who had received us with great luxury and refinement. She said: "Thank you, dear friend. Your soirée was delightful, but you must soon come to my place. You will see, it is absolutely sumptuous." Karl loved these worldly anecdotes and was naturally eager to assess her capacity for sumptuousness. Talking about her many houses, the woman had told Karl, "I have seven."

"I see," responded Karl, "and which is the main one?"

"They are all the main ones!"

And so of course Karl absolutely had to discover the palace of the woman-of-seven-houses. "As a palace," said Karl after visiting, "it was a quite ordinary mansion with crystal chandeliers and bourgeois carpets," meaning oriental carpets. But the woman had some surprises in store at her reception. Being Swiss, she had a cow, complete with cowbells around its neck, brought in from Switzerland and placed on the terrace overlooking the sea. Further on, a well-tuned choir sang Medieval motets a cappella. And the host herself enlivened the evening reciting verses from the Renaissance poet Louise Labé, all against a backdrop of the Mediterranean. Karl was enchanted, delighted, and laughing. "I have never had so much fun!"

Elisabeth adored Grand-Champ; she would have hated Monte Carlo. The famous Biedermeier furniture—remnants of a Hamburg past that Karl kept without ever knowing how to integrate them into his other houses, and which held absolutely no emotional appeal to his mother—ended up there in a "pretty, northern décor" with stripes on the walls in cold, formal manner. While the falsely palatial Vigie gave us room to play with style, that was not the case with Karl's first foothold on this very particular Rock. We had furnished the large apartment in the Roccabella tower with furniture Karl had found in Milan—Ettore Sottsass's newly hatched Memphis style, incomparable in its surrealistic freedom of design and color. We furnished the apartment in a day. It had a Disneyland atmosphere; everything was a game: the living room was a boxing ring, the bookcase akimbo, the desk like a pointed ironing board, the beds were flush with the floor, framed like pools you had to crawl into. Only the chairs and the square table suggested any sort of normalcy. The humor evoked by this universe of absolute style deviated from the overplayed bourgeois codes of this high-profile principality. The Memphis apartment was an eccentric instrument, perfect for communication but unimaginable for entertaining.

Karl complained that he couldn't draw in the hot and humid climate of the Rock. His hands were always moist and they stuck to the paper, even with the air conditioning cranked up. He informed me early on, "This is where I have to show myself, but I am going to work at Grand-Champ."

Time passed. A faithful habitué of grand Monegasque ceremonies, Karl stopped complaining about the heat. He had liked sunbathing in Saint-Tropez in his youth, but now, with his fan style, he was drawn into a strict rule of impeccable appearance. His image demanded it. When the dream opportunity of La Vigie came up, he believed he had been saved, when actually it marked the beginning of a long decline. Meanwhile, Jacques fled to the underworld of less princely cities, where the police were not so interested in him.

⁂

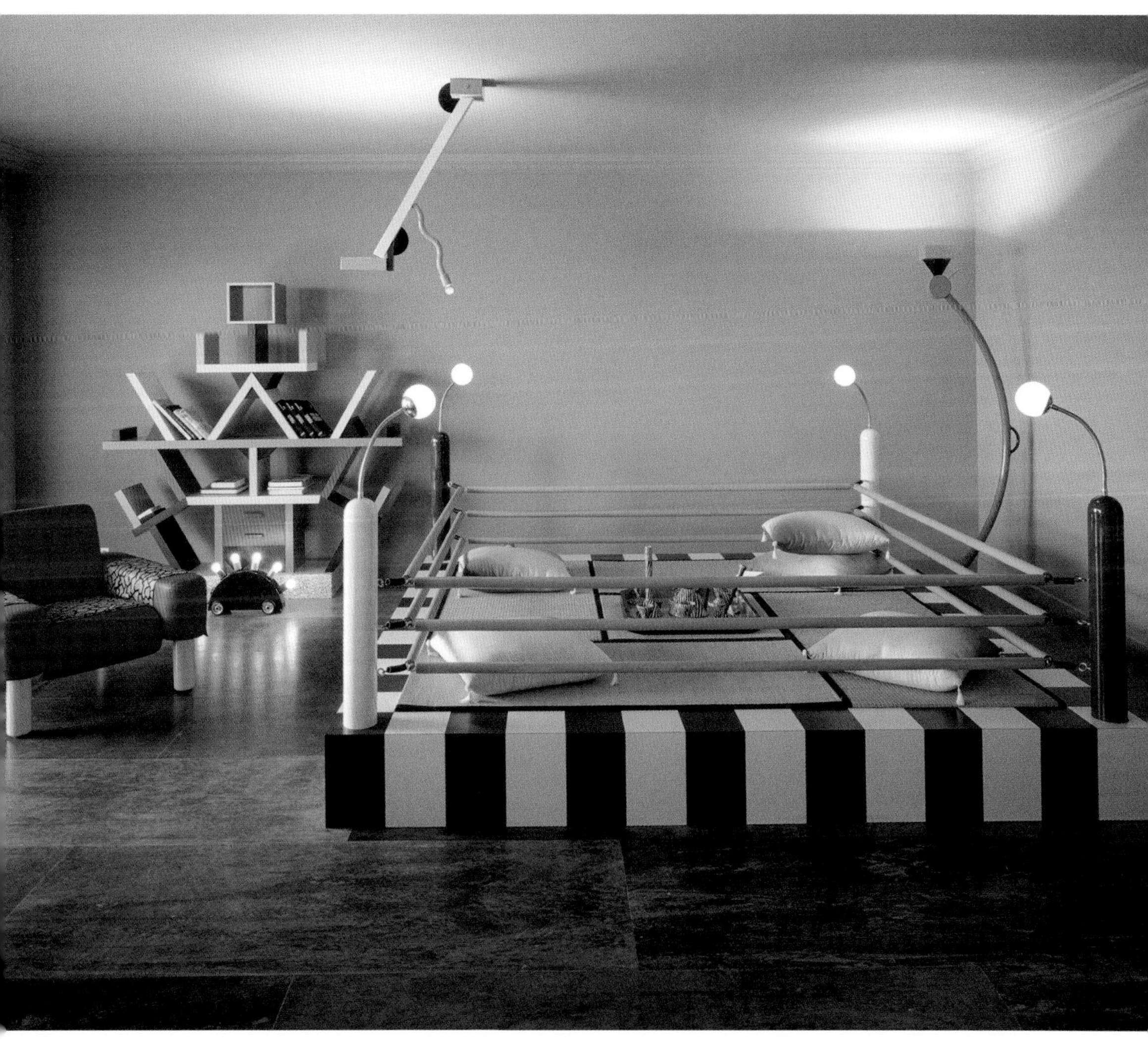

Memphis in Milan. Sottsass and his friends had created a fun, colorful, irreverent style. Karl couldn't resist the opportunity to devise an apartment that was "anything but bourgeois!" As he was quick to point out to all his visitors, "Without Memphis, I don't know what we would have done."

Jacques loved Karl, his mother Armelle, Proust, Rilke, and Diane de Beauvau, his fugacious but ever-true fiancée.

SEX AND DEATH

Jacques's great love was Karl. He had an unfailing admiration for him. He came to the studios regularly to help his friend with the famous "fittings," sitting in a corner to watch the session unfold. Marie-Louise de Clermont-Tonnerre recalled her surprise at Chanel one evening. On a flight with him, she had begun a petit-point tapestry to pass the time. That evening, in the middle of a work session, she saw Jacques doing embroidery, so as not to be outdone. He ended up giving it to an assistant, who finished it as a small, charming cross-stitched cushion, which Karl could put on his belly when he traveled, as was his habit. Jacques spent his time clipping out mentions, news stories, and articles in the press about his hero. He methodically filled countless boxes, which Karl discreetly referred to as "Jacques's business."

When Jacques launched his *Soirée Moratoire*, his fate was already sealed. Knowing I was somewhat reserved on the subject, I had been spared the details of all-out gay sex, which in this case, tragically, led to AIDS. Karl had dressed up like a wizard, the height of irony, alas. He laughed then, but he always liked to be in the right, and later sought my assurance: "Do you think Jacques's death is my fault?" Three times he asked me this question and each time I answered that he had nothing to do with it, wanting to soothe his conscience. But the more he asked me the question, the more I saw all those years when Jacques, prisoner of the money that Karl kept giving him, was slipping inexorably down a dead-end street. While I, thanks to Karl, could build houses, excavate the grounds to create pools, create sceneries, and explore new passions such as television, Jacques saw only the tiniest responses to his desires: a minor film for Fendi, the superb Venetian Ball at Le Palace, snatches of creative energy begging to be produced. He was called lazy, but he was above all a thwarted lover. At the beginning, Karl liked to indulge in sweet talk about sex, and Jacques played along, losing himself in his addiction to it.

One day, laughing as usual, and knowing that he was shocking me—it was not difficult— Jacques told me that he had put a chocolate éclair between Karl's buttocks and eaten it. Karl burst out laughing. I didn't believe a word of it. After that, Jacques spared me the details. But drama would come later, in our

Memphis apartment in the Roccabella. I had left my room to Anna, who had just arrived. Jacques's apartment was just across the landing, with a nice guest room, furnished with Thonet furniture in Secession style with very Viennese, Fendi stripes. It had two twin beds and I could sleep in either. When I woke up the next day, still under the covers, I noticed a shape in the other bed that didn't fit at all with the aesthetics of the room. The shape grunted and turned over. Some man, dressed in leather and chains, had gone to sleep in the bed next to mine without me noticing. I had slept well but the awakening was quite a shock. I quickly slipped on the traditional white cotton robe, the standard breakfast uniform at all Lagerfeld houses, and hurried across the landing, where a smiling and serene Anna was beginning her day. Seeing my disoriented state, she naturally wanted to know the cause and I told her what I had found that morning. We decided not to talk to Karl about it, but it was too late—he had a good ear and had heard everything. The rest of the day was a nightmare. Karl wanted Jacques out of Monaco right away. We did not see Jacques that day but heard Karl shouting all day, furious and distraught. I asked Anna if Karl was going to send Jacques away for good. "Of course not, he loves him too much," she said.

I had always been quite fond of Jacques and didn't want to know anything about his vices. He could not give them up. Karl was outraged, also for my sake; it was if I had been assaulted. He did not want me to be a part of it and we avoided talking about Jacques. Later, when Jacques was in the hospital, Karl told me that it was because of his liver, but I already knew that he was lost.

It was at a fashion show at the Théâtre des Champs-Elysées that I made the painful discovery. We were backstage after the event. The fashion mavens were delighting in Karl and his latest collection. Jacques was next to me, wearing a coat. I wanted to put my hand on his shoulder but it slipped down his back. Horrified, I felt the stark contours of his shoulder blade. He looked at me, I kissed him, and he smiled. Brahim, the chauffeur, had seen everything. He came over to me and said, "You see now." Brahim was my way to reach Jacques, as Karl never stopped saying Jacques was being treated for a liver problem and there was no need for me to see him. I knew Jacques loved the Tintin books and oranges I sent to him in the hospital, writing him words that did not need an answer. Diane, who went with Karl on his visits to the hospital, described to me Jacques's ordeal. I was in Le Mée one day when I saw oxygen tanks arrive. Karl told me that Jacques was finally coming home to rest. I saw the tanks, but I did not see Jacques. He did not want to stay there, the hospital was more appropriate given his condition. I asked to see him but Karl said, "You cannot.

The oxygen has eaten away his nose. It's horrible." There was nothing more to say. At the beginning of summer we went to Grand-Champ, Karl and I. He then spent the summer in Le Mée and I stayed there a few days with him. The summer passed slowly. Then one morning he called me, "Jacques... It's over." He was crying. Jacques had died surrounded by his mother, his fugitive fiancée, Diane, and Karl, his bitter lover. The Mass in the small village church was strange, with Jacques's family on one side, Karl and a few friends on the other, and the ashes divided in two, half for his family, half for Karl. All submerged in tons of white flowers.

Karl and I returned to Paris that evening. He had the little mahogany box with him and said to me, "Go find a vase, something that we can keep in the house. Put the box inside; no one will ever know." As luck would have it, I came upon a fountain a few days later, a large old urn painted to imitate marble. There was a little door at the back, originally there to access the plumbing, but it was the perfect size for Jacques's ashes and I placed him in the belly of the urn. I had to climb a stepladder to do it, because the urn was on a tall column, far from the curious. Karl was happy. Jacques was home.

I remember a lunch I had later with Jacques's mother and Karl in the intimacy of the grand salon in the Hôtel Pozzo, near a window looking out onto the park. We were in a corner amidst silks, velvets, and gold, bathed in the summer light. Armelle was wearing a gray flannel skirt and a rose-colored sweater, a few pearls around her neck, and spoke passionately about the Limousin cattle farm she and her sister were taking care of. With her smooth complexion, well-coiffed silver hair, pale eyes, and soft but firm voice, Armelle had a luminous, serene, and endearing presence. Karl said that she was the only person in Jacques's family that he liked. He also helped her in her muscadet vineyards and every day sent her generous baskets of the flowers he loved. None of us at that moment could picture the poor wretch of a few years earlier, dressed in filthy leather and dragging the chains around his feet, his neck collared like a dog, his eyes hollowed out by drugs, this lost and deranged Jacques that friends had encountered one night crossing the Île Saint-Louis. They had wanted to help him but were powerless; he was prisoner of his depravity, crawling back into his hell of sex and death. Neither Armelle nor I had any idea of this sordid descent. Karl said nothing about it.

It was only much later that I learned the truth of Jacques's slide into sadomasochism. He told the people he met, "I am being driven into hell!" But he was perfectly lucid among his cries of despair: he no doubt still loved Karl even as he fled from him.

I had no answer for Karl. He did not want to plead guilty but would still blame himself forever. Karl and Jacques, hapless lovers: the one could not give the other anything physical, only money to push him into the abyss.

Jacques died horribly. Karl survived without ever being able to free himself, or to love. He said to me, "I will tear out the pages." I was shocked. I said that he should not be so violent, that it was enough to simply close the book and put it back on the shelf. But I understand his pain today. He had seen Jacques weaken, deteriorate, his beauty eaten away by the devastating disease. He who had not seen his mother dying, nor his father, had been faced with the decline of his lover, whom he would have forgiven everything, even when he could not forgive himself.

⁂

THE QUEEN'S TEA

Antoine de Castellane, Victoire's father, had received the United Kingdom's Queen Mother at his Château de Rochecotte estate. When she asked "to wash her hands," he could not help blurting out, "Don't flush the toilet, we want to keep the royal pee!" This was exactly the sort of thing I wanted to avoid when she came to Grand-Champ. The château was being remodeled and the work had just begun. I had ordered woodwork panels for the rooms on the ground floor and there were a few pieces of furniture that had been brought from Paris. Everything was in disorder with half-unpacked crates and boxes everywhere. There we were at the beginning of summer, immersed in a mess: certainly in no state to receive royalty. But the exterior and park were nearly perfect. Karl's attitude was that gardens take longer to grow than woodwork and so we had to begin outdoors. That's what we did, giving the château new life after the death of Jacques.

Bertrand du Vignaud, who worked for the Caisse Nationale des Monuments Historiques, had proposed a visit to Karl's château from the Queen Mother, whom he knew well. Karl was so excited, the guest list had to be perfect. In addition to the local authorities, Karl wanted a close guard around him. Jacques's mother and Laure had to be there, as did Gilles, Bertrand, and me, of course. He also thought that André Leon Talley, the fashion star of *Vogue*, would be an offbeat and useful presence at the high-status event. When Bertrand caught wind of this he angrily explained to Karl that the Queen Mother could not allow a journalist to attend her social engagements in France. Karl insisted, but Bertrand held his ground and finally laid it on the line: "If you invite André Leon, she will not come." Karl of course cared too much about the visit and regretfully had to uninvite his American friend.

During the month leading up to the visit, he called me several times a day—the flowers, the cakes, the furniture—he was worried about everything. We thought that the south terrace not far from the entrance and overlooking the large pool was the ideal place to have this tea, not only for the light but also for the view it offered of the fountains, the sculptures, and the paths bordered with orange trees in planters. The gardens burgeoned with roses, but Karl nevertheless saw fit to add others, as Louis XIV did for his fêtes. Moulié-Savart, official supplier of Karl's houses at the time, had to fill two trucks and drive them across France. Rather than putting them in vases, the idea was to arrange the flowers in pyramids, like enormous wedding cakes. They were everywhere and the gardens were richly scented. We had brought out white vintage chairs, large white tablecloths, the appropriate white and gold china, and large umbrellas, also white. Everything was perfect—even the weather obliged by painting the sky a deep blue. Elizabeth Angela Marguerite Bowes-Lyon, Elizabeth II's mother, had only to arrive.

She did so, and at the appointed hour. We were deployed like little soldiers around Karl at the château gates, in front of the chapel. The motorcycle escort rolled up, then a few black cars, and finally the legendary Daimler—the iconic automobile transported every year across the English Channel aboard a Royal Navy ship to drive the Queen Mother on French soil—stopped in front of us. I will always remember the little step that slid out, like a James Bond gadget, before the chauffeur had even opened the door. She placed her foot on it and appeared before us in a turquoise dress printed with a large white foliage motif. As she made the famous royal wave I had the impression of a small Walt Disney fairy. As she toured the gardens alongside her host, she told him how enchanted she was. Walking in this marvelous garden was like walking through a painting, framed by flowers. Karl was smitten. We moved to the tables all laid out for the tea. Just in case, we had her favorite aperitif on hand, one she kept tucked away under the seat of her beautiful automobile, but this time she only wanted tea. Everything was going splendidly, but then, after a few cups of tea, something happened to mar the afternoon. The sky was clear, too clear: we should have been on our guard. A gust of wind suddenly swept through the garden with such noise and force that it lifted one of the

"She went through the Blitz in London during the war, nothing scares her."

garden umbrellas off its anchor. There were exclamations, frantic gestures to hold things down, but no reaction from the Queen Mother. Completely unperturbed, she looked at the offending umbrella and commented to Karl, "Oh, he gave me a standing ovation!"

After she had left, Karl said to us pragmatically, "She went through the Blitz in London during the war, nothing scares her." I had noticed that her hairdo, fixed to a turban that was the same color as her dress, also feared nothing. Karl added, "And that's not all, her earrings were also sewn to the turban." This woman was definitely not worried about storms. But most importantly, she had not asked to wash her hands.

⁂

GRAND-CHAMP, GRAND PROJECT

In 1990, storm Daria caused extensive damage to forests in France. Karl called to tell me that Rafael had assured him that the park at Grand-Champ had not suffered terribly. Of course Karl, who had seen the terrible damage to French forests and parks in the news, was quite anxious about that "not terribly." We left quickly to see for ourselves what the fury of the elements had wreaked on the estate.

The road to the château looked much the same, apart from a few large branches hanging here and there. But when we began touring the park we were stunned by the selective power of the storm, which had disrupted the harmony of the place in two precise spots, uprooting trees that were nearly sixty feet tall. The wind had pulled them out of the ground and snarled them together. Karl said to me, "It's incredible—it looks like they were put in a spin dryer." Strangely, it did not seem so much catastrophic as spectacular. Rafael was behind us and kept repeating over and over, "It's nothing. I'll take care of it. In a month everything will be in order and then more trees will grow." Karl was happy to hear such optimistic words and finally said, "All in all, we came out pretty well. The rest of the park hasn't been touched. Grand-Champ has always been lucky."

An enclosed forecourt with stone pillars was built in front of the entrance to prevent curious onlookers from peeking inside in the hopes of glimpsing the famous couturier. The orange garden was built next to it with a courtyard and gate. Rafael was delighted. I had provided the plans and he supervised the work carefully. Citrus growing was his favorite art; oranges, lemons, and grapefruit his passion. On the sloping land to the west, the abandoned orchard was dynamited and replaced with a large pond featuring powerful fountains and adorned with period statues to give a very Grand Siècle allure. Another large pond in the higher part of the garden to the east, ringed with a half-circle of lindens, marked one end of the grand allée. Other lindens had been planted in the upper garden, and finally the many sculptures we had recently bought were placed in the park. The result was beautiful and became a model for the modern French garden.

At one point an old tree, an ugly fir that Karl hated, was struck by lightning in a storm and fell on one of the outbuildings, effectively cutting it in two. We thus discovered that the stables and the groundskeeper's lodge had only been joined recently. With the chapel, this allowed us to restore better balance and harmony to the masses at the entrance. Karl could not help commenting, "It is the hand of fate. Like a magic wand, we rediscover the Grand-Champ of the Blévins and forget that of Monsieur Kraf."

Immediately after Jacques died, Karl decided that Grand-Champ would be his great work, that his house would be magnificent. Jacques had found the house and Karl's mother Elisabeth had died there. Progress on the park was quite advanced and we already had plans for a neighboring piece of land: a more antique and romantic vision, very Hubert Robert. It would have a pyramid and an obelisk, symbols of the ideal garden at the end of the Age of Enlightenment. But it was the château itself that was the object of our most impassioned conversations. I had shown Karl my remodeling plans. We were rebuilding the east wing, the one that had burned during the Revolution, and were doubling the main part of the house. The façade remained unchanged; the bulk of the work took place on the back of the building. The expansion of the central section had two advantages: it made it possible to create a spacious grand salon on the ground floor, like the one at Roche-Guyon, big enough for the famous tapestries of Esther, while upstairs, Karl now had the roomy atelier of his dreams directly adjacent to his apartment. He was enthusiastic about the idea and called me several times a day to discuss details, sending me sketches and plans he had envisioned; he was very caught up in the project. I had had the plans and elevations drawn up and I suggested he have a scale model built to get a clear idea of where the château was going. He asked Marie-Louise at Chanel to help me realize this beautiful project. The scale model is still there at the château.

In all of Karl's houses, there was only one answer to the question of books: shelves, shelves, and more shelves. Of course we had planned to furnish the château with a battery of bookcases, but Karl's eagerness to put his bookplate, his seal, his emblem, on the château was overwhelming and he asked me to quickly find a place to put several thousand books. The old stables, which were used as garages, had very beautifully framed attics. Painted white, the space was ample and modern. He had called his good friend Andrée Putman. They had known each other for a long time but were like night and day. He regularly criticized her, which she endured with wit, or he praised and congratulated her, which delighted her. Andrée Putman was truly his perfect accomplice in post-Bauhaus black-and-white-and-gray optical design. But unfortunately, he couldn't help making mean cracks from time to time, unbefitting a friend, such as "They say of Andrée: more man than *pute*."[2]

It had gone over very badly—Andrée knew that "they" was Karl, who couldn't control his tongue. But that day the atmosphere was cordial. We were in the new lofts in the stables where I had installed the fifty or so wheeled bookcases that Andrée had produced. Design and intelligence, functionality and modern lines, all combined perfectly on the light-colored floor and created a delightful dissonance in a space that had once been the realm of straw. I had given it a very New York layout, but as yet no book had taken up residence. Andrée was ecstatic; Karl was overjoyed. And then we heard Andrée's deep voice, "Karl, this is too beautiful as it is, you must not put a single book in here!" Karl was stunned. "She is crazy." Later he added that the idea for bookcases on wheels, which she had claimed as her own, was actually his. As for me, I spent quite a few days liberating all the books from their boxes and putting them on the shelves.

In Paris, our purchases of works of art were going well. Grand-Champ was going to be magnificent. It was a vision, but unfortunately one that had not

2. *Pute* means whore in French.

been put down in writing. Karl began to betray Madame Pompadour to spend more and more time playing courtier to the princes of Monaco. And we were happily fitting out La Vigie as a princely resort, without realizing what poison lay hidden in this breach of faith.

⁂

LAURE AND ANOTHER FRIEND

Radiant, intelligent, captivating, generous, and, above all, loving to laugh, the woman who took the reins of power at Sotheby's—and who would take her fight all the way to the European Court of Justice, Treaty of Rome in hand, to give foreign companies the right to sell in France—Laure de Beauvau, née Rougemont, was a kindred spirit to Karl. They were both born in September under the sign of Virgo, which was also the sign of Louis XIV. Laure had been recently widowed when she met Karl: her husband Marc, Prince of Beauvau-Craon, had died a few years earlier.

Sotheby's auctions were held in the prestigious setting of the Sporting d'Hiver in Monte Carlo. Karl and I were beginning to restore La Vigie and to buy eighteenth-century furniture, tapestries, paintings, and sculptures for the Hôtel Pozzo, motivated by a desire to create an exemplary collection. We certainly did not lack for topics of conversation in this area. Karl and Laure were each impressed by the other's culture. He spoke to her about German culture of the Enlightenment and she responded with Russian culture, which she knew well. She was also passionate about Chateaubriand, about whom Karl knew little. When La Vigie was finally ready to receive guests, Laure was the first I invited. Karl was in Paris, scheduled to arrive the following day, but still hesitant to sleep in this new Trianon he had so coveted.

The opinion of a woman in a house is precious, even indispensable. Women always see what men do not. When I woke up the next morning I went down to the grand salon. It consisted of an enfilade of three rooms. The only furniture was a pair of gray-lacquered sofas, positioned at either end, otherwise the rooms were empty. The furniture would arrive later. I can still see Laure, sitting very straight, very princess-like, reading a book on the sofa facing the sea. She noticed my surprise and explained, "I love to sit in a salon." Karl arrived later that day, happy to learn that Laure and I had not been tormented by ghosts. He wanted to invite the entire Sotheby's team.

Exploring the grounds of the villa, I found an old path on a steep rocky slope descending to the sea. It must have been built at the beginning of the century and then abandoned. The descent was dangerous, and particularly thorny; a well-sharpened machete was essential equipment. But it was well worth the trouble. Those who dared discovered cement benches fashioned to look like trees, and small terraces under tamarisk trees bordered with turquoise faience balustrades. At the bottom, there was a fairy-tale private beach sheltered by an enormous rock into which a cave had been dug. Just a stone's throw from the Sporting d'Hiver, we were suddenly transported to the realm of Robinson Crusoe.

One of the first people I shared my discovery with was Stefano Casiraghi. He was delighted and enthusiastically described it to Karl, who said he would go down there as soon as an elevator had been installed. Laure felt the same way, but her team were not so willing to wait and were eager to explore the new territory. Dominique Doucet, Laure's loyal friend, took part in the adventure. She could not resist exploring the cave but got pricked by sea urchins. It took me a long time to extract all those dreadful spines.

In Paris, Laure took us on another adventure with all her customary passion. Her husband had been president of La Demeure Historique. After his death, Laure had remained very attached to the association, which promoted the restoration of the most beautiful French houses. Karl got involved as well and every year we summoned experts, historians, and heritage consultants to award two prizes. One was for the restoration of an eighteenth-century work of architecture, the Blondel Prize, in honor of the theoretician of pleasure palaces under Louis XV. The other was for the preservation of a park or garden dating to the same period, the Lajoue Prize, named after the rococo painter of imaginary gardens, whose works Karl avidly collected. The jury sessions filled an entire morning in the Salon Bleu of the Hôtel Pozzo, where Bertrand Vignaud brought us the selected dossiers. Laure was enthusiastic, knowing most of the owners. Daniel Alcouffe, punctilious as always, made remarks worthy of his status as a great Louvre curator. Liliane de Rothschild examined the dossiers with a keen eye and sharp wit. Pierre Lemoine, who had taken over Versailles after Van der Kemp left, was very adept at putting everyone on the same page. Alexandre Pradère, a master researcher on antique furniture, and Bruno Pons, his counterpart for woodwork, brought a touch of youth and additional erudition to this brilliant company. After much work and deliberation, we were treated to lunch. Bruno Pons identified woodwork from the Tuileries Palace in the dining room, recovered after it was burned by the Commune. Maurice Aicardi was also present at these sessions; together with André Malraux, he had conceived the law on donations of works of art. There was nothing but luxury, beauty, and erudition here. Karl was delighted to be able to forget for a while what he called his fashion "factories."

We often went to visit Liliane in her Paris mansion. She was happy to have Karl return her dessert plates, a porcelain service once belonging to Madame du Barry; she had put a label on the back to poke fun at the overcurious: "*petit curieux*" [little snoop]. But her real treasure was the key to the chapel at Versailles, which she proudly displayed to us. (The key has now been returned to the château.) Laure was very attached to Versailles. Her sister, Anne de Rougemont, worked with Olivier de Rohan at the Friends of Versailles association. We thus had the privilege of a very intimate visit to the king's house in a small group. During one of these visits Karl missed a step on the chapel stairs and found himself in Liliane's arms. She laughed at his distraction and exclaimed, "Karl, stop thinking about me!" To make up for his literal faux pas, he sent her a huge basket of flowers the next day. When Baron Élie, Liliane's husband, whose reputation as a womanizer was well known, saw the flowers he said, "It's another gift from my wife's lover." Another time, Laure wanted to go to Marly-le-Roi. It was my brother, historian of ancient literature, whom Liliane called "Monsieur de Saint-Simon," who welcomed us to the estate. The pavilions of Louis XIV had disappeared, but my learned brother was able to bring them back to life. Karl asked about his dear Palatine and the great Saint-Simon and my brother answered all his questions. From then on, Karl was a permanent member of the Saint-Simon society. He and Laure were like the Sun King and Madame de Maintenon here.

But Laure was wary. She confided one day to Alexandre Pradère, "Karl has an annoying tendency to turn on his friends, to start quarreling and bickering after a few years. I would like to protect this friendship." Unfortunately, her words were prophetic.

Some time later, heroine of the art market war, Laure became president of Sotheby's. She was hesitant at first, but Karl himself urged her to accept the challenging position. But once she had moved into her office, she defended the company like a mother defends her children. Karl was not happy about this. He complained that she had become too infatuated with the auction house. "She has become boring, all she talks about is her sales. Myself, I like to buy but I hate to sell." Alas, the worst was yet to come. A few Decembers later, alone at his house in Le Mée, Karl was expecting her to join him for Christmas Eve but she called to tell him that her mother was very ill and she couldn't come. That left Karl alone for dinner. When I arrived for lunch the next day and didn't see Laure's car, I asked him what was going on. He told me of his dreary evening, but when Laure arrived later, she soon had us laughing as always.

Three days passed. Karl called me and told me he had broken with Laure. "Her mother may have been ill, but I am told Laure was celebrating and laughing it up in Monte Carlo with a bunch of fools. Word gets around. Too bad for her if she doesn't know how to lie." He had never liked Christmas, and now Laure had knocked the angel off the tree. She sent him a letter to calm things down, but a few months later, when Sotheby's inaugurated the Charpentier Gallery across the street from the Élysée, Laure had enlisted the renowned decorator François-Joseph Graf. Karl had wanted me to do it. I told him it was not important at all and he responded, "You are wrong, it was yours to do and Laure has missed a golden opportunity." While the whole affair left me completely indifferent, he weaponized it to "wage his war," as he put it. The outcome of this gun fight: Karl, in need of money, had to sell his beautiful collection and had no idea how to do it. Furious with Laure, he called the rival auction house, Christie's, to do the job. He did not want me to help them, and the sale did not go the way he had hoped. Now furious at Christie's, diplomatic relations took a new twist: he called Sotheby's to sell a number of art deco works. Laure found out and asked to see him. He received her in Elhorria, all smiles and excellent Bordeaux; he knew how to please her. But Laure was not fooled. After her death, when Sotheby's published a book in honor of its former president, Karl refused to give them a beautiful photo he had of her. Indulging the old grudge nevertheless brought him little comfort.

There is an amusing epilogue to this story, now that neither Laure nor Karl are with us anymore. The organization responsible for the inheritance of Monsieur Lagerfeld's estate asked Sotheby's to arrange the prestigious sale of all his possessions. This was where Laure had the last laugh. And as the ways of life are infinite and mysterious, Pierre Mothes, whom Karl greatly admired and who had supervised the inventory of his big sales at Christie's, is now at Sotheby's in charge of this sale.

⌘

PIERRE AND GENEVIÈVE

An ironic eye always on the lookout, nothing escaped Pierre Hebey, whose spirit animal was the owl, the wise Glaukopis of Athena. There were two people who could be perfectly honest with Karl: Jacques, whose life was too short, and Pierre, whom Karl admired as much as he feared. Pierre advised, Pierre wrote, Pierre was an invaluable lawyer and a learned essayist. Pillar of the Éditions de la Nouvelle Revue Française, collector of modern sculptures and paintings, he was an advisor to Max Ernst, whom he collected, but was also passionate about the discoveries he made at flea markets. He and his wife Geneviève often invited Karl to their house in Biarritz in the summer. Pierre loved to hear Karl's puns but eventually got annoyed with the "fashion genius's" insistence on showing off his new Elhorria house, not far from their own. Karl would give tours of his house again and again at each visit, like a child showing off his new toys. Pierre stayed downstairs and grumbled, "Oh no, he's not going to do it again?" The women invited to the Hebey's were always pretty and sometimes famous. Karl, grand gentleman he was, wanted to honor each of them and had huge baskets of flowers sent to each. One day Pierre found his lawn covered with a dozen baskets of flowers and could not help exclaiming, "Where's the body?" Yet he often tried to help his friend out of tricky situations. This can't have been easy because Karl presented Pierre with so many conundrums. But he also gave him a lot of attention—"Too much," said Pierre—like the time he had a minivan fitted out with all sorts of extra features for enhanced comfort. He invited Pierre to get in but Pierre got carsick and ended up taking a cab.

It is impossible to talk about Pierre without including "Belle Geneviève," as Karl called her. She was a soothing presence in his life. "Geneviève is a haven," he liked to say, adding, "She's a woman I could have lived with." She had countless friends, a generous smile, eyes that put the stars to shame, and a halo of blonde hair, all perfectly complemented by light-colored outfits. No detail was out of place, she was impeccability in person, Karl's dream. She always loved Karl and was quite sad when her turn came for the inevitable falling out. Pierre was ill and Karl did not want to see him anymore. Nicole Wisniak asked, "Pierre, are you saddened by Karl's attitude?" Pierre, ever the philosopher, answered, "No, I know him. I am sad for Geneviève."

Karl had forgotten that day in London when they were tired and Geneviève had dozed off in the car. He had tenderly rested her head on his shoulder, a very rare gesture for a man who shunned affection. He had forgotten his exact words when she told him that she had loved Max Ernst, but he had responded, “Then you have loved two Germans.” But in the depths of his solitude, six months before he died, he remembered that he loved her. When someone remarked how beautiful she was in a certain photo, he responded, “Geneviève is always beautiful.”

Karl shared with Catherine Deneuve the minor flaw of often being late—“always late” said Pierre, regarding both. The day he organized a lunch to introduce them to one another, Geneviève wanted to be on time but Pierre dawdled. When they finally got to the restaurant, they found the two renowned latecomers happily talking to one another. For once, they had both arrived on time.

My mother had a small house in the Basque Country but efforts were being made to dislodge her. Karl told me to see Pierre. Pierre saved my mother and I will always be grateful. When Karl and I finally “divorced,” Pierre said to Karl, “You were wrong to separate from Patrick, he brings good luck.” Pierre was very superstitious.

⁂

Karl admired them: the photo he took of Pierre and Geneviève Hebey is simply perfect.

Laure had an irresistible smile. Here she is framed by Karl and me with our neatly knotted ties.

Guy Bourdin had asked to put the lovely couch from Elisabeth's room under the apple tree in the orchard. Years later, in the depths of the château, I found her ashes hidden behind it.

Slowly but surely, the small château became more and more splendid. It was our grand project and we discussed it every day.

On a royal visit to Grand-Champ, amidst pyramids of macarons and flowers, Britain's Queen Mother conversed with Karl. She likened her visit to the gardens with a stroll through a painting. He was delighted.

"This is how I envision my room at Grand-Champ!" you wrote when you sent me this drawing, enthralled by the new projects we were always developing.

There was serious intent behind all the play and certain questions were constantly on his mind: "What room will I sleep in? How can I set up a studio worthy of the place?" Every day he drew new plans, but when I finally got the idea of doubling the main building, he was overcome with excitement, "That's it, we're there! We have to build a model!"

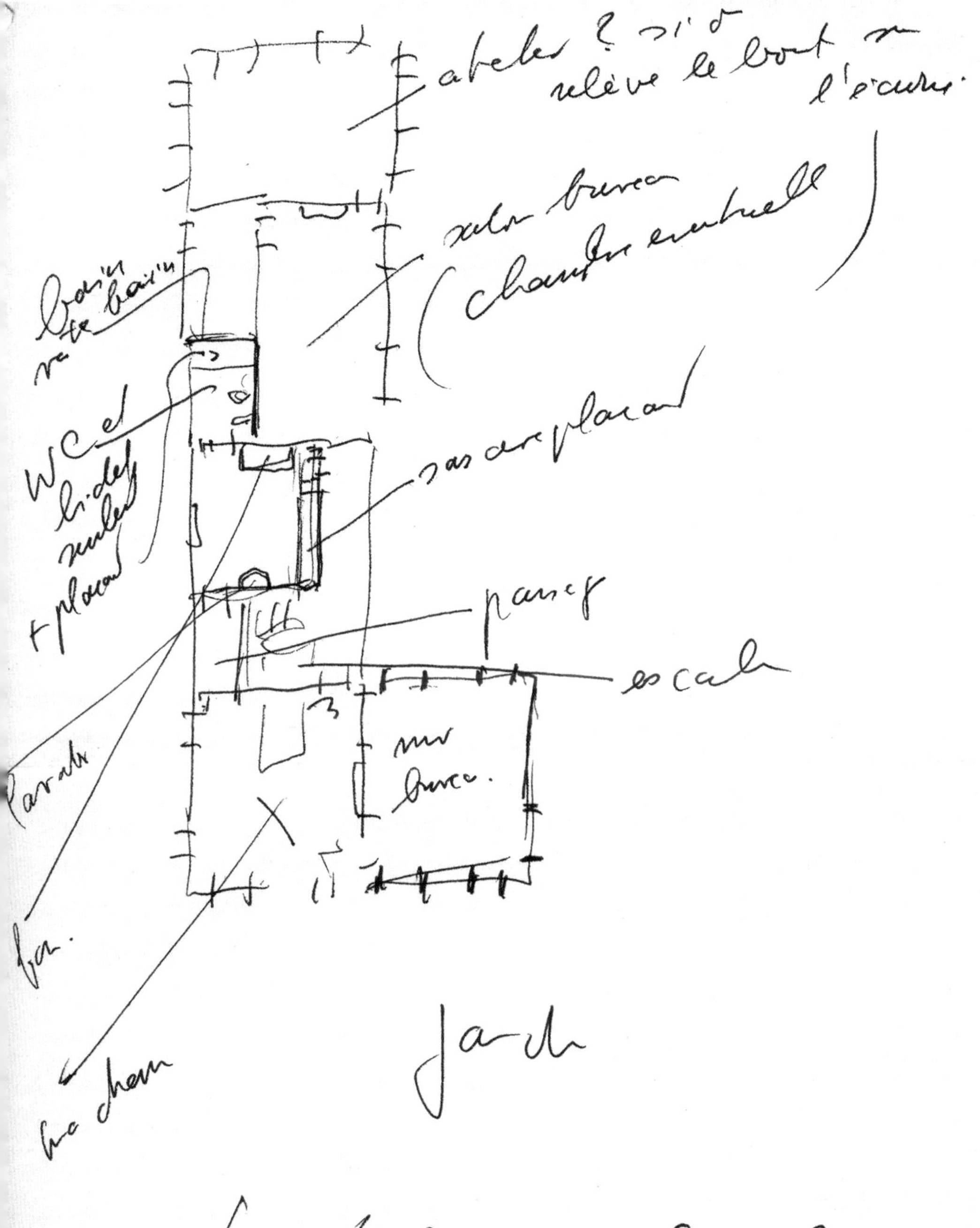

atelier ? si on relève le bout sur l'écurie

salon bureau (chambre éventuelle)

bain et bains

WC et bidet, meubles + placard

sas avec placard

passage

escalier

mon bureau

lavabo

gaz

vers chem.

Jardin

Je pense que commencerait si bien les lieux te plaisent lire le plan.

Karl's libraries contained his entire cultural universe, demonstrating his insatiable curiosity. He was quick to embrace new interests, including the latest technology.

CULTURE

You told Pépita, journalist at Paris Match, *that you were "appalled by the poverty of current vocabulary: sympa, super, génial, cool..." to which we could now add "top." It is clear that you were disseminating your culture of historical literature via the magazine: the sermons of Bourdaloue, the prose of Saint-Simon, the letters of Madame Palatine. You were experiencing exciting moments and enriching exchanges with scholars, connoisseurs, or simply people who shared your culture outside of the fashion world. It is clear that you wanted to spread this culture, to transmit it. It is a pity that most of these desires remained at the level of vague ideas, like when you said to Pépita, "I am working on a biography of Princess Palatine," adding, "for pure pleasure, because I will probably never publish it."*

Your craving for books led you into such diverse realms as classical literature, modern literature (Léautaud was a landmark for you), art in all its forms, and finally biography, the lives of the men and women who fascinated you. You shared this passion with Jacques. Culture, for you, came mainly from others, from your curiosity to meet them. Of course you shunned introspection, good old psychoanalysis; instead you praised intelligence, which you saw as the solution to all other problems. Freud said, in reference to Leonardo da Vinci, that he may have transmuted his sexuality at a young age into a "drive for knowledge." You did not like psychoanalysis and used television programs and other interviews, whether lying down or sitting, as a vast form of manipulation, intended to strengthen your communication. But the quest for power and knowledge that seems to have guided your entire life might well be explained by your strange lack of sexuality. Encounters with your intellectual equals became more and more infrequent over the years. Caroline was one of the exceptions. We had thrilling, enriching moments and conversations revolving around culture and learning, but you replaced it with the deliberately frivolous world of fashion. The world you considered to be part of your "job" consumed your daily life, all your time. And while there were encounters with artists, architects, and other captivating people, these moments were brief and you inexorably returned to the world where the following day was all that mattered, the world of fashion always going out of fashion.

I cannot forget the words you said to me one evening after a dinner we had organized at the Hôtel Pozzo. I had laid the table with an exceptional array of trellises, vases, and sculptures, an entire miniature French garden in glass, porcelain, and papier-mâché, a rare work crafted in Italy in the late eighteenth century. You had organized the dinner for the leading names in fashion of the day. Their prattle at the dining table was nothing like the thought-provoking questions that Anna or Laure might have posed in similar circumstances. When everyone had left, you congratulated me on the centerpiece and said, as if to apologize, "You see, only you and I can understand this. These idiots will never understand anything!"

⁂

THE HOUSES

"The one who has two houses loses his mind."

— ÉRIC ROHMER

It was your favorite quote and you loved to throw it out like a prophecy every time you bought a new one.

We were doing extensive work at Grand-Champ, buying furniture and art all year round to decorate that dream house. On top of that, you were also interested in new houses. We ended up looking at houses as objects, objets d'art, of course. You would ask, "A house? To do what?" And you would answer, "A house, you have to know how to bring it to life, to occupy its tiniest recesses, every space must have its reason." Reading, working, and, of course, eating and sleeping well—for you, every function had to find its place here. Houses were our great passion: you loved project sites, and I loved designing them.

LE MÉE

Houses are Karl's soul... Yes, but not this one.

This small charming house had nothing of a château about it. You said to me, "Look, it's not far from Paris, we can fill it with all the things we have in excess while we wait for Grand-Champ to be ready. You can bring your dog and I can set up an atelier." There was a small detached house that could be used for that purpose. The house was surrounded by a broad lawn, with flowerbeds on the side facing the outbuildings, where the vegetable patch was. One side of the house was very French-eighteenth-century, which, not surprisingly, you liked. But we had to forget about long walks here. We had to get in the car for a nice stroll in the woods. The village of Mée-sur-Seine was actually at the edge of a sprawling suburb. I understood only later why you wanted to set up house here. Jacques, who had started shooting a film in the garden, was being treated in Garches—it made the trip easier.

The simple lacquered white furniture was perfect for this dollhouse. The rooms, although not very big, were light, with large windows. I played all day long with the terrible Yunes, Diane's insatiable son. She had gotten him back thanks to Jacques, her ex-boyfriend. And while I took care of Yunes, she went to visit Jacques in Garches, with you. Unhappy days. You had added some plasters, sconces with monkeys in palm trees, Serge Roche rococo. But I had a hard time helping you make sense of this house. When you found a large wooden armchair with a matching footstool, you thought the garden was done. You claimed it was an eighteenth-century Venetian gondola seat. I made no effort to research that, merely content to procure copies to complete the garden décor. The beautiful Ines de la Fressange posed on it to advertise your famous taste. The magazines were promoting all your creations at the time. You had invited the Labros for the weekend by asking Françoise to do the shoot. I lent my room to Philippe, who wanted to write. You had silhouettes printed on fabrics and had cut out others; we were in a world of puppets. You wanted us to paper a stairway with Bécassine illustrations; it was a toy house, a showcase house. It was actually all very conventional, "amusing" as you said, and a bit silly.

But those times were hard for you and I can still see you in the late summer sun, leaning over the little table in the garden, your papers and beloved pencils around you, drawing—to distract yourself, you said—magnificent illustrations of a naked king for Hans Christian Andersen's Emperor's New Clothes. *Between visits to dying Jacques, you gave the best of yourself. No, this was not a happy house. The dogs were certainly the happiest ones here; this house was not at all for you.*

When you sold it later to Caroline and Ernst from Hanover, it was finally returned to its true purpose: only a family could bring life to this house.

LA VIGIE

La Vigie began as a big worksite. There was no question of our living there before it had been restored, let alone decorated. The stairway was my main concern. The work was heavy, tedious, and costly.

Sir William Ingram, an Englishman who made a fortune in printing ink, built La Vigie in 1902. Only an Englishman could have envisioned a mansion hanging over the sea, like in a Lorrain or Turner painting—a completely unique sight in the principality. It was a dream for you and you realized that dream. While we were working, decorators—socialites, needless to say—presented you with fabrics, each more printed than the last, and you ended up surrendering to a sprinkling of small flowers on a white background. It suggested to you Liotard's suavely Levantine pastel decorations. We did an entire room with that print: a large room, it was transformed into an enormous cup of fruit yogurt. The pattern was dwarfed by the space. Of course that did not stop Laure from sleeping there under her pleated canopy. As you will remember, when the house was ready, I slept there alone, cradled by ghosts who hadn't seen a human being in over fifty years. I asked you to come, but you were not so brave and I had to turn to Laure to inaugurate the new palace. She, too, got along very well with the ghosts. William Ingram had disappeared at sea and the beautiful Vigie had long slumbered until it became ours. The Société des Bains de Mer of Monaco ended up buying it. Princess Antoinette came a few times to lead rescue exercises for the Red Cross, but the house was falling into disrepair and you were finally offered a fabulous long-term lease. Of course it was up to you to restore the estate. The stairway, all the windows, and many other parts had to be redone, while the triple salon on the ground floor was very impressive, but not well balanced. I had large Corinthian columns installed to cadence the space. The library, indispensable in all your houses, was of Russian and Swedish inspiration. The salon upstairs was decorated in red damask and gilded furniture, very Rothschild, so that Liliane would not feel too out of place. We slept in canopy beds, brought in period furniture and precious paintings, and amidst all this luxury you did not forget Jacques, who was no longer with us. A room decorated in Gothic and Moorish exoticism à la Pierre Loti, with pronounced Duc de Morny dandyism and a few paintings to inspire dreams, was waiting for he who would no longer come. Trianon was to the countryside what La Vigie was to the sea—it would have been completely incongruous to have come there in a bathing suit. But looking back, I realize you didn't have much space to work in. There was a desk in your room, but when it was hot, the paper would stick to your hand. As it happens, you never said anything to the prince, and once again the magazines gave you publicity that you didn't need because the taxman was watching. You aptly called it "La Côte d'Usury."

VILLA JAKO

Villa Jako: a picture postcard with a bitter taste. A false memory of your irretrievably lost boyhood in the posh suburbs of Hamburg, on a hill overlooking the Elbe on its way to the sea. You had the gift of finding original, out-of-the-ordinary houses. It was no doubt a madman who had built this house in the north of Europe, looking like a temple with a Roman atrium as its entrance. Once through the door, we encountered a basin cut into the marble floor. In the designer's mind, it evoked the impluvium in an ancient Roman domus, but transplanted from sunny Italy to the rainy Baltic, the idea had lost some of its appeal. We found it quite amusing. A glass canopy had been installed to prevent flooding, but what about the hole? There were pros and cons. Of course I insisted on saving the exotic invention. In Hamburg we visited our lovely Florentine Pabst and ate peeled shrimp with a spoon. I loved it.

"You know the eighteenth century well, but here we have the culture of Mitteleuropa, which you do not know, it's not your department, my dear!" That's what you said, gently mocking me, when you mentioned names like Bruno Paul, Richard Riemerschmid, Bernhard Pancok, or the Darmstad School. Of course, it was all it took to arouse my curiosity, and I quickly learned about all of them. Thanks to you, I discovered this whole pre-modernist aesthetic universe which was preparing the future Europe. The ideological and methodical Jungenstil was not the art nouveau of sweet, and, in many ways, more romantic, France. During a trip to Vienna with Franck, the friend who would bring scandal, I discovered an enormous hanging light fixture at an antique dealer, an embossed ogive covered with what looked like bubbles, white bulbs that animated the strange golden sculpture. The fixture, perhaps by Dagobert Peche, another creative mind you revealed to me, came from the marble foyer of a theater in Vienna from the Secession period. When I showed you the photo, you wanted to buy it right away. It was to be hung in the center of the grand salon, where it would be more appropriate than Borek Sipek's crystal flights of fancy that infatuated you at the time. We were in the midst of arranging the house when the doorbell rang. An older gentleman was at the door, delighted to see you and talking constantly about a reunion, hanging on you like an old friend, "Mein lieber Karl, wie gehst?" *You were*

visibly embarrassed and spoke even more quickly, barely introducing him to me. After a somewhat awkward conversation, you saw him back to the door and said to me, "He met me when I was young but I don't remember him." Then added, "At least he's nice." My skills in the language of Goethe had remained rather weak since high school, but I had clearly understood the man speaking about the school where you played together in your distant youth. The past catches up with you when you least expect it; old classmates are dangerous in this respect. This was undoubtedly a decisive argument for abandoning that house. "In the end, it was a dream of the past, but I have nothing to do here, my life is elsewhere. Besides, I don't even know where I could work." To the press, you cited the cumbersome ghosts of your parents, even though they had never slept there.

Later, the idea of creating a new perfume, a posthumous tribute to Jacques, led you to compose this absurd photo where he stands next to you with his back to the camera; Jacques was never one to turn his back to a camera. As for the Viennese chandelier, you took it to the Basque Country. Vienna in Biarritz, why not? An amusing idea.

ELHORRIA

The Basque Country was my summer home. As a young stylist you were invited here by the De Mouy family, to Jean Patou's house in Biarritz. The region reminded you of Brittany, which you had left for good. What's more, Biarritz was the home of Geneviève and Pierre Hebey. So when you were offered this large house with its characteristic Navarrese style, you wanted to chart a new life there. Our relationship was falling apart but you insisted on showing it to me. Dominating a hill, it was very 1930s, on a beautiful, long, and narrow estate. It was very beautiful and was called Elhorria, which means "thorn" in Basque; it must have had a colorful history. The dark brown timbers stood out crisply against the white walls. You loved that graphic effect, remarking that Basque houses had something in common with Japanese houses: each side of the house was a façade in its own right that played off asymmetries. There was even a spacious patio, more Spanish than Basque. Inside, a grand staircase and a gallery provided a nice anchor for the pleasant, modern rooms. You wanted to install Liaigre furniture there. It was very much in vogue, and created in the same dark colors and straight, solid lines as the exterior. In short, you had almost nothing to do and could just settle in. The only problem, a fairly annoying one, was a dull roar coming from the highway below. You had the idea of installing a pool with a powerful jet of water to drown it out, but it was a rather far-fetched plan that would only have replaced one noise with another.

You used to invite male models there and amuse yourself photographing them splashing naked in the pool, spending a lot of time and energy on it, as was your habit. But you ended up selling the house to seek the summer sun of the Saint-Tropez of your youth, when you played with Antonio and Juan, recalling the sex symbol you never could be.

Basque proverb:

"Leben hala, Oraï hola; Guero etchakin nola." *("Once like that, now like this; later I don't know.") This is how you lived those days.*

⁂

MISSED HOUSES

With all these famous abodes, you were still drawn to new dream houses. But after the first visit you woke up.

LA GORDANNE

"One of the major Swiss monuments": this is how this small neo-Palladian masterpiece on the lake between Geneva and Lausanne is described in the Switzerland travel guide.

We had all gathered at the Hôtel des Bergues in Geneva. Diane and Jacques spent their time in bed, receiving guests as if in a salon, naked as jaybirds under the sheets. We laughed a lot; you suggested the Orangerie at Versailles for their wedding. Their minds worked together quite nicely. Diane had the necessary madness to amuse Jacques and the regal bearing to make him dream. Of course Jacques already envisioned aristocratic, wealthy, Catholic progeny. But these two had to get dressed, because you and I were impatient to discover this house that was for sale.

The Palladian inspiration was perfectly realized in this round villa. With its temple-like portico composed of a simple pediment on a majestic colonnade, it was a tribute to Goethe. Inside, its grandeur and intimacy evoked the intrigues of Jane Austen. A stairway followed the curve of the wall up to the bedrooms. You found your room, another one for the lovebirds, and designated a third for me. The property extended all the way down to the lake, but there is always a hitch in every nice story. Here, it was a road that very inconveniently blocked access. Jacques went back to his underworld, Diane went back to her life, and you said nothing. The beautiful Gordanne was sold to a Greek shipping magnate.

JOSSIGNY

Dame Anna Wintour had commissioned you to do a reportage at the beautiful château of Champs-sur-Marne. The decorations of the Marquise de Pompadour enchanted you and inspired you to take fashion photos. Not far from there was a small house that a local scholar had pointed out to you. It was like a miniature Grand-Champ, containing the sort of carved woodwork we dreamed of. It was the work of the famous Nicolas Pineau, whom Catherine the Great had summoned to Saint Petersburg. You made an offer to the curator of this historical monument that was most unacceptable to the ministry that owned it: you would undertake all the work, add a few pieces of furniture from your collection, and after having lived in it for a while, you would return it to the State. Your audacity did not pay off; the State wasn't interested. Then your car slid on the ice and was damaged. You concluded that "it was not the right time." On my part, I hastened to find comparable woodwork for Grand-Champ. Jossigny, a pretty eighteenth-century folly, would remain a mere anecdote.

⁂

La Vigie, this picture-perfect dream mansion, was all too real. It taunted him as he looked out from the modernist balcony of his apartment in the Roccabella tower. He was overjoyed when it was offered to him, but it would turn out to be a poisoned chalice.

La Vigie was reborn after years of abandon. I had columns installed in the salons, while Karl had created these oversized sofas, upholstered like one of Queen Victoria's carriages. Alfa Castaldi, Anna Piaggi's husband, took this photo of us. Karl is drinking Coca-Cola from his beloved Lalique glass, while I go on with my incessant studies.

Elhorria was a Basque mansion, or perhaps more a collage of several Navarrese houses with a Spanish-style patio added on, a very sophisticated extravagance in a folk style. Art deco reigned here. It brought back all the memories of Jean Patou's house in Biarritz and Karl loved to show it to visitors.

Friends came to Le Mée to comfort Karl after Jacques's death. Françoise Labro managed to capture a Caillebotte-like atmosphere: large sun umbrella, Borek Sipek wicker chairs, cashmere boutis *while taking tea. While Karl shows his drawings to Pierre Hebey and Philippe Labro, Geneviève and I talk about other things.*

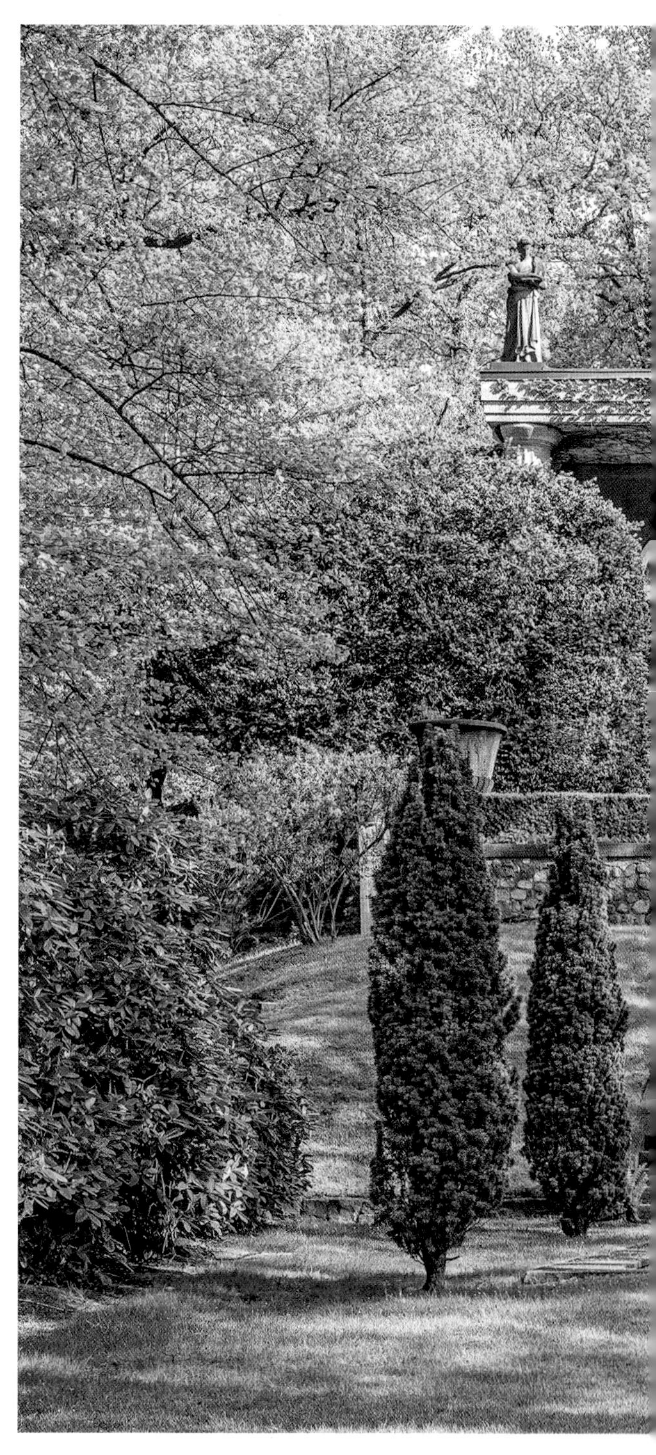

Villa Jako, a temple to the glory of reconstituted memories. It held all of Mitteleuropean culture, at least as Karl imagined it.

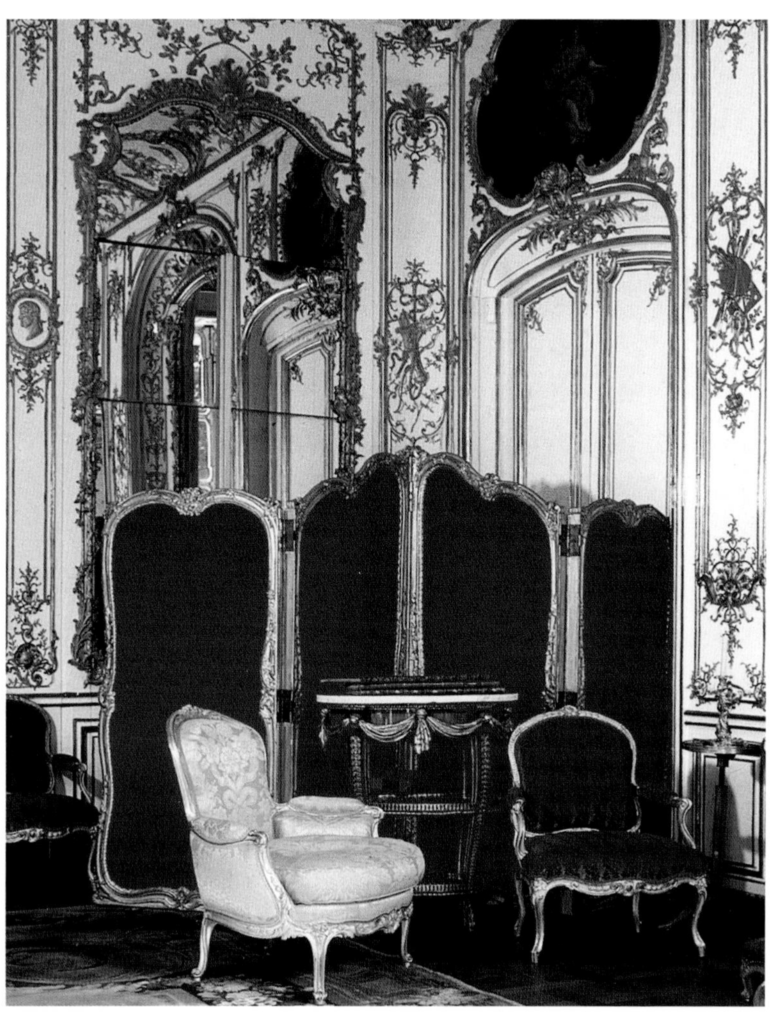

The fully restored salon, classified as a historical monument, features Madame Pompadour's banquier screen.

The large painting by Fragonard in the office. It is now in an American museum. The terracotta statuette on the right is now exhibited at the Louvre.

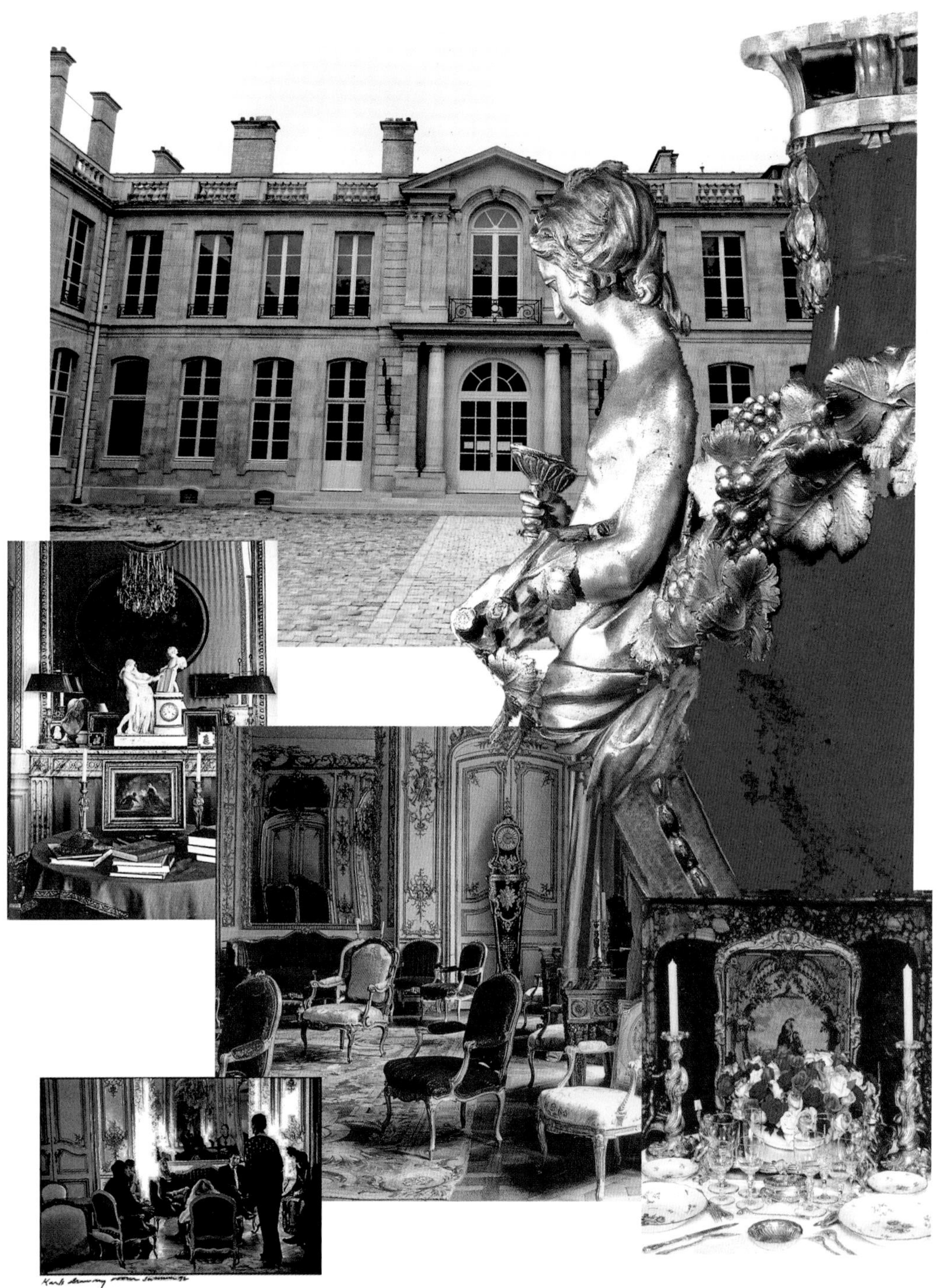

Our move into the most beautiful part of the Hôtel Pozzo was an apotheosis. We restored the original giltwork in the salon.

SPLENDOR AND PARANOIA

Robert de Billy had just died. He had lived on the ground floor of the Hôtel Pozzo, so coveted by Karl. The grand salon was classified as a historic monument but was very dirty. I began by having it restored. A very nice surprise was in store for us: under the old paint, we found the original ceiling decorated in gold leaf. The restorers got to work but soon had to be taken to the hospital. The cause? Lead poisoning—the old paint was rich in it. Masks had to be worn to finish the job. The results were so spectacular that Jean Ferré, one of the most demanding inspectors from the Monuments Historiques, ended up congratulating us. The chandelier was hung, he passed underneath, raised his arms to gauge the proper height, and looked at me with a smile. He was delighted and so was I.

Our purchases of works of art had never abated and the house was quickly furnished. Karl was eager to move in. Completely renovated, the kitchen was under the direction of a cook and the old stone vaults that had made it so characteristic had been restored. A stairway led down to the wine cellar, also under a vaulted stone roof. I had set up a room there to store photographs, Karl's latest passion. I also had a whirlpool bath installed, a dry massage tub—the latest in waterless thalassotherapy—and a tanning bed, which he used very little.

His room, hung in gourgouran silk with broad green stripes, was just off the grand salon. At the back of the room, two large screens created an alcove with an immense painting by Fuseli, a fantastic *Deluge*, over a large bed. The subject was strange, as is true in many works by this painter: a woman seeking help in the catastrophe, but only one hand was visible, with six fingers. Could this detail have troubled our friend? A little while later I began to notice changes in his behavior. He used to go out freely without a care but now wanted bodyguards on certain occasions. His room was huge and overlooked the park, so it was inaccessible from the outside, yet he claimed that he needed a weapon to defend himself. Monsieur Jouannet, a very serious man, had replaced Brahim as driver. The latter had been fired, under the pretext of his having opened a pornographic film store. The truth is that during the final years of Jacques's life, it was Brahim who brought him soup, the only food he could eat, in his

"You want to be a fashion designer, my son, but you are no snob, so you should be a supplier!"

last home, under the roofs of Rue de Rivoli. And later, it was again Brahim who took Karl to Garches each day to see Jacques in his agony. Witness to the grief that Karl sought to escape, he had seen and heard too much. But Monsieur Jouannet was irreproachable and Karl must have found him reassuring. He gave Karl an electric stun cane that could be kept next to the bed. If attacked, he just had to seize this magic stick and press the button—thieves beware! But it was only a tiny sparrow that finally startled him, and he nearly broke some of the wonders in his collection with this formidable weapon.

But something else soon disturbed him, this time over his head. Vivien Clore, son of the billionaire Sir Charles Clore, was renting the large apartment above Karl's and was in the habit of treading noisily at night on a very Versailles floor. Karl wanted to offer him a carpet to muffle the sound.

Patience, soundproofing, and an expiring lease would finally resolve the issue: the second floor was eventually vacated. There was no doubt that Karl would abandon the ground floor and move his bedroom upstairs. Downstairs it was replaced with a salon that could also be used as a dining room. There were two large salons upstairs. The blue room looked like a state apartment but was also used as an office. It was inspired by Choiseul's decorations on a Van Blarenberghe snuffbox and had a large Turkish bed installed in an alcove behind two columns. There was also a yellow and amber room furnished with enormous sofas and matching armchairs. Both rooms had paintings crowding the walls all the way up to the ceiling. At the back there was an ample gallery with a large table that made a good atelier where each fashion house could have its own well-defined space. And there was a huge storage room already filled with furniture waiting to be sent to Grand-Champ. Karl was delighted. From the cellar to the piano nobile, he had almost eleven thousand square feet all to himself—and all of it was used. He was quick to inform his visitors that "not one inch of space is wasted." I had to remove a sauna installed by the previous tenant. Karl could not stand the heat or the idea of wearing only a towel around his waist. The bathroom was sober and spacious, with a large round mirror by Ruhlmann, Karl's favorite. But even greater sobriety lay next door in a room with gray woodwork, deliberately Jansenist and austere with its steel officer's bed. However, this asceticism was short-lived, to be banished by the discovery of a magnificently carved bed by Georges Jacob.

The objects, furniture, and paintings we had amassed were now beyond counting. The inevitable sale that came later catalogued no fewer than 1,130 lots, but there were many other things that were not to be sold.

⁂

FASHION, I HATE YOU

"You want to be a fashion designer, my son, but you are no snob, so you should be a supplier!" That startling line was attributed to your mother and disseminated your entire life through countless interviews. But I doubt Elisabeth actually talked to you like that when you were young. All the things your mother said about you are mostly inventions on your part, to suit you. The fashion in Hamburg after the war was simply the fashion of Paris that had fascinated you in the pages of Le Figaro. *She had a subscription back then. The names of the great couturiers—Dior, Chanel, Schiaparelli—did not sound like "suppliers" but rather like the creators of a new art of living. These words actually reflect more your rejection of your profession. You kept finding your dear colleagues uneducated and unexciting. You did not hesitate to say, "I raise the bar, don't you think?" Later on, fashion designers became creators, but never artists in your eyes. When Bergé championed fashion in museums you replied, "Fashion in the museum? A ridiculous idea, we are only* torcheuses de chiffons.*"*[3]

However, drawing was at the root of your destiny. But here again, that anecdote, probably fabricated, about the director of the Hamburg Fine Arts

3. "Chiffons" are rags or scraps of fabric. A *torcheur* is someone who works quickly and carelessly. But Karl uses the feminine form *torcheuse* to suggest the gay world of fashion design. The image is that of effeminate creatures that throw rags together.

Academy, whom your mother consulted when you were a child to hear him pronounce that you were better at drawing clothes, is all the more insidious because it forced you, from the start, to narrow your creative ambitions. Here again we find your low esteem for the profession. But you could not have had this brilliant career in the world you criticized so much without your remarkable imagination and dazzling erudition. Right from the start, you gave your best, with your crystal-clear convictions. Your absolute guiding light would be Oskar Schlemmer, Bauhaus artist who revolutionized the vision of the human body before the war. The Schlemmerian silhouette—broad shoulders, narrow waist, and rounded hips—has always been your ideal. Poiret, 1920s graphics, and the Gazette du Bon Ton *completed your ideal of fashion. When you designed the costumes for Schnitzler's play,* Countess Mizzie, *you realized your dream. Your creations for Chloé were unquestionably the peak of this style, where graphics dominate the garment. Later, when you had to find a new trend for Chanel, you worked on this style as if it were an application, a simple app in your computer-brain; you personalized Coco and it was a revolution. You developed applications without end, you could create as many different fashions as the brands asked for. You could make a pastiche of all the creators of the day on demand. The Chanel style was a game where you excelled; the Chloé style a passion.*

I remember early on that you would sometimes start with an idea and then, two or three days later, you would throw away all your drawings and start again. But later you were more convinced right from the start. Apprenticeship in style is an exercise of vision, and there you got faster and faster.

An emblematic piece of Lagerfeldian advice: "The brain is a muscle, the more you work it, the more it produces."

The great ritual of fashion is the presentation of the collection to the press, nowadays increasingly digital, but at the time very physical. The sets that you liked to invent became for you the inseparable scenery of fashion, the music the aural cosmetics for the event. At the end of each show, after the swarm of journalists, stylists, and other hangers-on of the catwalk had shuffled by to compliment you, your thought was always the same: "That does not give me the next one!"

Two collections, four collections plus one, or two more for the same house in the same year... your calendar was overflowing, because you collected fashion houses like you collected houses to live in. And you got on very well with both, and in both.

You were doubtlessly aware of what was happening, you realized over time that you had set up a machine for creating fashion. The design studios would soon displace designers, who were doomed to oblivion, still receiving some parsimonious tributes in museums, or in vintage sales for those nostalgic for a world where glamour was king.

Today money is king and fashion is an application.

⁂

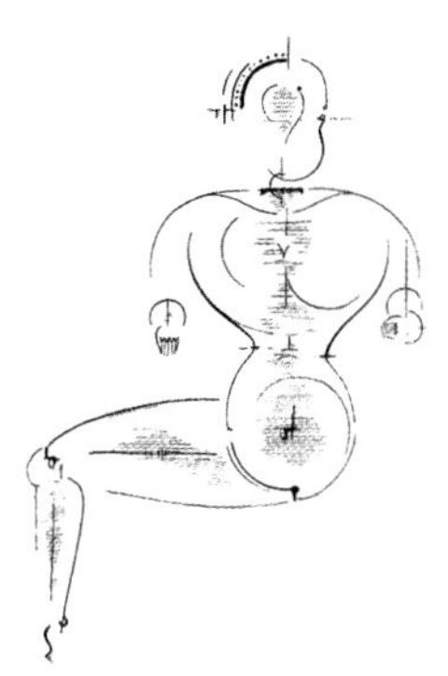

Chloé, Fendi, Chanel, and then Lagerfeld, not to mention all the extras. Karl designed everything—he knew how to produce styles the way others produced novels, complete worlds in themselves—but his appointment at Chanel to take Coco's place was the high point of his career.

Marlene was known the world over; Karl was a mere debutant stylist. Well before his appearance on Rue Cambon, Marlene asked him to make her a Chanel-style jacket. He blew this chance and that was the end of it, witnessed by his handsome and loyal assistant, Gilles.

Gilles
Karl 84

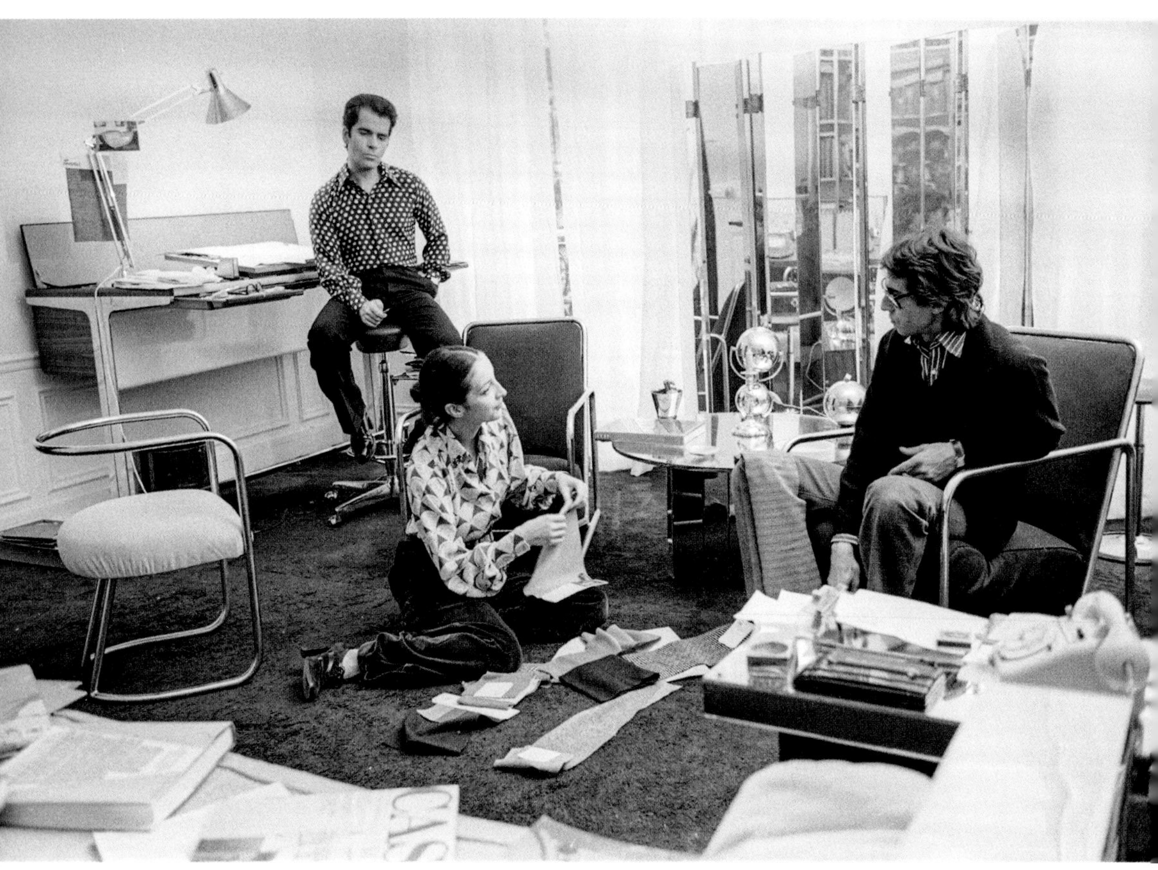

On Rue de l'Université, Karl had created the first modern influential fashion studio. The discernment of Marie-France Acquaviva complemented the creativity and insatiable curiosity of Gilles Dufour. They were a perfect duo and contributed to Karl's success at Chloé.

Vincent Darré needs no introduction: Instagram has made him a star. He made Karl laugh and Karl forgave him almost everything. And he knew how to do everything, as long as it was not ordinary.

le 23 2 2000

From the top: Hervé Léger, Eva Campocasso, Camille Miceli, Sophie de Langlade, Carlyne Cerf, and Victoire de Castellane. All angels who helped Karl immensely with their smiles, laughter, and originality.

THE ANGELS OF WORK

Karl kept telling me that work was a source of life and he was happy to get down to work. Whether it was fashion or photography, his assistants—dedicated, attentive, at times a touch critical, but usually enthusiastic—were like guardian angels to him. He loved them, he enjoyed their company, he treated them like friends and considered them as such. There is a long list of the angels who made it possible for him to produce all that he did. I can't name them all, but I remember many of them well.

THE ARCHANGEL GILLES, MARIE-FRANCE AND THE FIRST ANGELS

Gilles Dufour was a young man with fine features who always had a friendly smile, complementing the line of his almond-shaped eyes. Very polite and attentive to others, although naturally shy, he had asked Pierre Bergé if he could come to work with Yves Saint Laurent. He was told that he was not "professional" enough for such an important position. Not discouraged, the young fashion enthusiast met Karl Lagerfeld in the Parisian atelier of François and Claude Lalanne, an artist couple who were becoming very fashionable at the time and who sold their works to Saint Laurent and to Karl, among others. Karl immediately recognized Gilles's qualities, his curiosity for everything, his ability to learn quickly, and the way he brought back the best information with unfailing positivity. Gilles was always attuned to the world and able to translate essential influences into grist for fashion.

Karl knew early on that he had to create his own atelier outside of Chloé, which did not allow him to have an assistant. And so it was at his place, Rue de l'Université and then Place Saint-Sulpice, that he judiciously created his workshop of ideas. He paired Gilles with a lovely young woman, the image of a Renaissance Madonna, wise and knowledgeable in the art of clothing, Marie-France Acquaviva. For his first collaboration with Chloé, a luxury fashion house created by the vibrant Gaby Aghion, Karl designed just one dress; the house employed many other designers. The following season, he designed three, and three years after that he became the exclusive creator for the brand. Marie-France, who was also a Chloé model, immediately fell in love with that first dress and wanted to present it. She would be Karl's first assistant. She was not a socialite but very inspiring for her femininity and natural elegance. They worked together wonderfully. Karl guided them the way he wanted to go and Chloé became the theater of Karl's triumph, opening the doors to fame.

His success grew with every new collection and new proposals continued to arrive, but Karl could not respond to all of them. There was one brand with a very French name that was particularly insistent: Marie-Martine. Karl told Gilles to handle the request. And there, the demon of possessiveness, which regularly reared its head, once again managed to get the better of him. Returning home one day, Karl had the taxi driver take a roundabout route down Rue Saints-Pères so he could see the Marie-Martine windows. He turned to Jacques and me and declared furiously, "You see? Gilles has copied me once again!" He did not dare, of course, say it to Gilles's face. He wanted Jacques to convey the message that he should not copy Karl. Karl was not very brave in that respect.

But this episode did not stop him from turning to his dear assistant for new adventures, which were in no short supply. Cinema was a source of inspiration for Karl. With Gilles always at his side, he regularly dressed actresses such as Marlène Jobert, Anouk Aimée, or Stéphane Audran. The latter introduced him to Marlene Dietrich. Later, after getting angry with Stéphane about a stupid problem of money, he claimed it had been his mother who introduced him to the Blue Angel. This is quite improbable since Elisabeth Bahlmann shunned those circles and had never met Marlene.

Marlene received Karl and Gilles at her place on Avenue Montaigne. The pretext was the Christmas edition of *Vogue Paris*. She was dressed in a body stocking with a leather apron so she could work in the kitchen, which she loved doing. The apron concealed a well-placed slit that allowed her all the necessities without having to undress. Helmut Newton, photographer of fashion and nudes, who dreamed of seeing Marlene one day, eventually got his introduction thanks to Karl. She received them seated on a sofa with the apron hiked up. Helmut, who had spent his whole life fantasizing about female sexuality, sat paralyzed like a fool and blurted out to his idol, "It's true that you have lovely legs!" She threw him out.

Marlene's dishes are still famous. Karl and Gilles both had the chance to savor her Wiener schnitzel, breaded cutlets with green beans and carrots. But the star was worried about something. She was to receive the Legion of Honor and was proud of it. Karl offered to dress her for the big ceremony. The basic garment was a crepe sheath, but Marlene wanted to wear a Chanel-style jacket over it. This was our friend's first foray into that realm. Marlene was used to being dressed by the grand Mademoiselle herself and knew all the secrets of a Coco Chanel tailleur by heart. Karl found a fabric in tones of green and black that suggested the famous tweeds of Rue Cambon but was merely horrible plagiarism. Worse yet, he had never looked closely at the construction of the famous sleeve. Marlene pulled it on as if it had been made by some kind of wicked fairy seamstress and declared the jacket unwearable. The novice fashion designer took offense and didn't want to see her anymore. And, as was to be expected, after that he only said the most horrible things about his former friend.

He would get his revenge much later with Chanel and here again would find Gilles. But he initially asked Hervé Léger, a very serious, very professional young man, to come help him create his first collection for Rue Cambon. Karl liked Hervé a great deal and was distraught at his untimely death. But at the time, Hervé was a bit too calm for Karl's taste. Knowing how to mix fire and ice, he went looking for a whirlwind at the Studio Berçot, a diabolical school of fashion led by a strong character, Marie Rucki. The tornado's name was Eva. The world is small enough, the fashion world even smaller: Eva was the niece of Marie-France, the wise Madonna of the Chloé collections. But Eva was the complete opposite of her aunt. She created, and still creates, jewelry pushing the boundaries of the imagination. Eva is the emblem of the crazy fashion that took hold of Paris in those years.

VICTOIRE, DEMONIC ANGEL

Karl did not get off to an easy start at Maison Chanel. The first critiques made it clear to him that he had to rework the elements of his atelier-laboratory. In a corridor he discovered Victoire, "not beautiful, not even close," he told me, but an explosion of mischief and insolence that immediately won him over. Their exchange was brief and to the point.

"What are you doing here?" he asked.

"I work in the printing department preparing invitations."

"Forget that and come with me."

She did not hesitate to follow this extravagant person, who told her, after she had posed for Helmut Newton, "Above all, do not eat red meat before a photo session!" He sent her to Virgin and FNAC to buy records, 33 and 45 rpm, to make the soundtrack for the fashion show. This would later be the work of the famous Michel Gaubert, star DJ of fashion events. At the same time, Karl asked Gilles to come help him change what he called the "old fusty brand."

Irony of ironies, Victoire de Castellane was Gilles's niece. Gilles chuckled as usual and Victoire burst into fits of infectious laughter. She was an intoxicating cocktail of upper crust insouciance." The new team was on its way to revolutionizing the "proper" Chanel suit and its unflappable pearl necklace.

Ondes de choc

Karl wrote these words—"shockwaves"—on the edge of a desk for a song that would be recorded by Victoire, who was sitting on the floor: "*Je bouge comme si j'étais sur pile / chaloupe des hanches, fais des ravages et je m'en balance / J'ai pas le coup de rein végétarien, fais gaffe à toi, mon p'tit Lucien.*" [I move like I'm on a battery / I sway my hips, wreak havoc, and don't give a damn / My hip thrust isn't vegetarian, watch yourself, my little Lucien], adding "*Travaille ton corps que je l'explore*" [Work your body so I can explore it]. It was a whole scene, and Monsieur Desrues, a respectable man who had lived well and been making very pearly, golden jewelry for the famous maison since Mademoiselle Chanel, would never get over it. Victoire did not dress Avenue Montaigne but Pigalle. Tutu and leather jacket with nothing underneath, all on towering heels: this was how the new muse of the studio presented herself, advancing toward Monsieur Desrues so he could try her latest haute couture jewel-belt on her lovely bare belly. The extreme, oversized or very small, was more than normal for this sassy young woman, this antidote to depression, the antithesis of the too-calm Romy Schneider. The pearls became gigantic, the discreet "CC" that had reflected off the golden buttons of the elegant now became large letters boldly displayed on the most unrestrained of accessories. And added to that was an explosion of the brightest colors orchestrated by Uncle Gilles.

Adding spice to this theater of humor and creative madness, young women arrived from everywhere to take part in the revolution, although the chosen ones were always up to Karl. When Camille arrived, Karl put his hand on hers and said, "I knew your mother well." Camille worked in the editorial department; her allure and joie de vivre enlivened Rue Cambon. She had a hard time leaving Chanel, and Karl was never happy that she left. She ended up designing for Vuitton and Dior. Sophie de Langlade, who had been an editor at *Vogue* and worked with Guy Bourdin and Helmut Newton, accepted Karl's invitation to run the press office at Chanel. Sophie lived her life the way she wanted; she left to work at Dior while pregnant. Later, Karl, who loved this freedom in Sophie, as well as her intelligence, asked her to come to direct Lagerfeld, his own brand—rather astonishing for one who once told me, "I would not like to have my own name on a piece of clothing." That made me smile—Elisabeth would have been proud of it. And I have always kept a sweater he gave me bearing his name. But Mademoiselle Chanel, who had always defended her name as if it were a noble title, would have been devastated to see all the different troublemakers that Karl attracted into her cherished studio, not to mention her legendary style being edged out by the "CC" look. One of the many unexpected guests at this cenacle of fashion was a young girl, still in school, who came regularly to help with fittings, invited by Gilles and Victoire, her sister. She was ready for anything, even just picking up the pins. She was always laughing. Karl nicknamed her "Princess Mathilde" and gave her a red satchel. Mathilde Favier cut her teeth in this atmosphere and is now famous for her brilliant smile and good humor, the joy of the house of Dior. There was no shortage of cheeky visitors to the studio, which offered a very young Sofia Coppola a position managing shoes (so we may better understand her *Marie-Antoinette*). A journalist, the bubbliest of the bunch, joined the party and did not want to leave the fitting sessions on Rue Cambon. It was Carlyne Cerf de Dudzeele, the queen of patchwork, the funniest editor on planet Fashion. Since then, she has continued to spread the triumph of Chanel's liberation all over the world, a fashion that bursts into laughter, that speaks to new generations and forgets the old advice regarding what is proper and politically correct. It was with this studio that Karl won the battle of fashion; a page had been turned. He also brilliantly demonstrated the leading role of the "workshop-studio" where the synergy among young inventive talents was worth much more than a great creator cut off from the world, always needing to have the upper hand in everything. The demiurge acted through interchange and sharing, marking the great turning point in this industry, which is still evolving today.

VIRGINIE, ANGEL LIKE NO OTHER

A clever young woman, Virginie Viard, a tall brunette, a little reminiscent of Marie-France Acquaviva, Karl's first assistant at Chloé, arrived in the middle of this dizzying maelstrom. She was dependable and would soon become indispensable in the construction of the new style developing at the crazed studio on Rue Cambon. Virginie provided the wisdom and rationality Karl needed to realize the smallest details of his rich and sometimes eccentric collections. He quickly grasped the importance of his discreet new assistant, saying, "She is my right and my left hand." History is often written with an implacable logic and it is now Virginie who holds the reins left by her late hero. Her style is like her, feminine above all, but also with the sense of efficient construction that Karl taught her.

Karl hired, trained, and inspired many vocations in the incredible number of assistants he had at the various fashion houses. I could not name them all, but there was one I found quite amusing: Éric Wright. Tall, slender, and seeking elegance in every instant of his life, he listened to Karl with boundless admiration. At each fitting, his famous response was taken up in chorus by the studio: "Karl you are a geniuuus! Karl you are a geniuuus!"

VINCENT THE DEVIL AND THE ITALIAN SISTERS

Pierre Hebey had strongly urged him to be nice to the new president of Chloé and Karl promptly pretended to pinch his ass. "You asked me to be nice to the gentleman," he retorted. It was the same gentleman who introduced Vincent Darré to Karl, although Vincent needed no introduction. He was a friend of Pierre and Geneviève Hebey and well known around town. His reputation as a tireless party animal preceded him. And when Monsieur Moufarrige asked Karl to look at Vincent's file, Karl laughed and nudged Vincent, "Ah no! I know where this kid comes from the Studio Berçot!"—Lady Rucki's factory of wild geniuses. Vincent was hired but soon got bored—he was not suited to the fashion house's timeframe; his nocturnal revelries were not compatible. At night Vincent flew off on wings that no doubt inspired his creativity, but he was left yawning early in the morning. Karl caught on quickly and already forgave him everything. He apologized for waking him when he called in the morning. Even if Vincent, his head in the vise of an overwhelming hangover, told Karl he had to hang up so he could go puke, Karl found nothing to complain about. He found the perfect job for him and sent him to Rome to work with the Fendi family. Paola, Anna, Franca, Carla, and Alda, the five sisters who had inherited a small saddlery business from their father, were devoted to Karl, the hero, who created an empire for them and gave them the monogram that would make them famous all over the world. I remember Karl toying with the possibilities offered by the letter F, finally pairing it with its rotated self in yin-yang fashion. He said to me, "You see these two Fs, they are like the Fendi sisters, each one does what it wants but cannot escape the other." Each quite different, the sisters had a deep sense of family. Anna had to leave for New York, and Vincent went with her, visiting stores and flea markets. He found an enormous trunk that he wanted to bring back. The trunk was somehow shuttled back by various means and ended up in Rome. Now Vincent had to get it back to Paris and Karl found himself packed into a minibus with his assistant and the object in question. "Ah yes, you and your big finds!" grumbled Karl, although he certainly found it amusing.

"You see these two Fs, they are like the Fendi sisters, each one does what it wants but cannot escape the other."

And then it was Vincent who rescued the soirée of Franca Sozzani, editor of *Vogue Italia*. She had invited Eartha Kitt to a grand gala evening. The singer was as unknown as she was incongruous among the peninsula's bourgeois circles. Miss Eartha, whom Orson Welles declared the most exciting woman on the planet, had begun singing, but her inimitable accent and gravely voice were not an immediate hit with this morose audience. Dear Vincent had been medicating his boredom with a good dose of alcohol and suddenly climbed onto the table in front of Karl. He waved his napkin in the air (and even hit on the head the formidable Suzy Menkes, oracle of the New York fashion press, who had dared say some mean things about the Fendi collection) and joined Eartha in her famous refrain "...and an old-fashioned millionaire." His enthusiasm was contagious and the audience finally let loose and starting singing along, waving their own napkins. At the end of the evening, Eartha came to thank the party animal for his help. Karl had to admit that his insufferable assistant was sometimes very useful.

But the Italian adventures were not over yet. Vincent had found a gorgeous young man, lost in Paris and without papers after fleeing Cuba. His name was Mario. Vincent kept asking Karl to let him take Mario to Rome with him and the young migrant soon found himself on Mr. Lagerfeld's private jet en route to Rome. The arrival at the small private airport should have been relatively uncomplicated. However, at the last minute, storms forced them to reroute to Fiumicino, with all its associated immigration controls. Karl took the lead at the checkpoint, waving his iconic fan in one hand and his famous forged passport in the other. The cordon of police melted away, applauding him. Meanwhile, his assistant and the fugitive came through as simple luggage.

Vincent loved to go bargain hunting in all the flea markets of the world. And when he excitedly brought his mentor his latest find from London—a parachute

"Moschino n'est pas un style, c'est un pastiche!"

with all its strings and rings—Karl envisioned making a dress from it for Chanel. But then what had to happen happened. Vincent, who could not stay long in one place, accepted a recent offer to become the fashion designer for a young Italian brand, Moschino. Karl initially seemed to be okay with it, but a day came when he wanted Vincent at his side—strangely enough, the same day that Vincent was to present his new collection. Vincent pointed out the coincidence and Karl could not repress a "*Moschino n'est pas un style, c'est un pastiche!*" Vincent took him at his word and asked Karl to write it down and sign it. Karl was delighted to oblige and Vincent had the statement by the famous—and famously mean—couturier printed on the clothing of his new brand. It was all that was needed to ensure its fame. Karl, Vincent thanks you once again.

⁎

THE BEAUTIFUL DRAMA

Karl Lagerfeld had only won the coat contest. Yves Saint Laurent triumphed in evening gowns. It's like comparing Olympic golds in the 400- and 100-meter hurdles. The rule was not to let anything show. Yves had talent, Karl had genius—or the other way around depending on which admirer you are talking to in this opportunistic milieu. Among small circles of friends Karl made it known that Yves was "nice, but not too bright." He would also add, "Let us not speak of his culture, which is limited to Cocteau and a superficial reading of Proust." With each new collection he awaited the opinions of the authorities of the fashion press—John Fairchild for *Women's Wear Daily*, Hebe Dorsey for the *Herald Tribune*, and all the *Vogue* people, some of whom lived for fashion like André Leon Talley, Carlyne Cerf, and Madame de Wintour—and seconds after the end of the Saint Laurent show, he knew everything. “Ah yes, he has still glued Cocteau to his dresses; this is not fashion but an intellectualism of rags,” he would say, immediately adding, “Anyway, he always makes the same dress.” But after his exploits at Chloé and Fendi, planetary success awaited him at Chanel, and at that point he forgot all about Yves.

On the day of Yves’s funeral, Sophie de Langlade, Karl’s Lagerfeld brand manager, seeing her boss arrive at the studio, said, “Karl? You’re not at the funeral?” Karl responded in his usual rapid-fire manner, “Come on Sophie, you know we were mad as hell at each other.”

He was more worried by Pierre, Pierre Bergé, the business genius, without whom Saint Laurent could not have existed. Pierre who “had it in” for Jacques, which delighted Karl, but also Pierre who bought and collected masterpieces, which Karl was naturally quick to dispute: “His Goya is a fake, just look at it!”

What he did not know, and did not want to know, was that Pierre, a remarkable bibliophile, had a superb collection of books. Karl was extensively schooled in northern European history and literature, while Pierre collected the masterpieces of French literature. Karl bought dozens of books every week, exploring their content and adding them to his store of knowledge. Pierre scrutinized every corner of the book market to acquire rare pearls that the Bibliothèque Nationale would quickly preempt for sale. This was where the conflict lay: two minds with clashing passions. While Jacques played some part in it, the antagonism between these two men was mainly a question of their intelligence and their education. Karl could not reduce Pierre to a simple, worldly amateur. While the sale of Karl’s art collection in Monaco was a nice success, the sale of Yves and Pierre’s collection (Pierre’s mainly) was a triumph. This sale of the century brought in 373.5 million euros. Karl could not countenance the fact that this feat so greatly surpassed his own. He ruminated against the dealers who, according to him, had taken advantage of him, the auction houses that had failed to do their job. But how to respond? Not even the masterpieces of Philippe de Champaigne could bring in the price obtained for Matisse’s *Les Coucous, Tapis Bleu et Rose*, which sold for nearly 36 million euros.

Over the years, Karl had decried the taste of Rue de Babylone with its Lalanne furniture, which he compared to poorly made plumbing. But the basis for it all was more museum-like and contemporary than Karl would have liked to admit. During all these years, Karl had been interested mainly in the decorative arts. With me, he had indeed built up an extensive collection with more than a thousand pieces of furniture but also a great number of historic paintings of fine quality by the likes of Champaigne, Fragonard, Boucher, and Hubert Robert. In the end, it was the only true collection he built up in his life.

Conclusion: Pierre was stronger, financially.

⁂

KRIEMHILD AND NEMESIS

You always told me, "My favorite heroine is Kriemhild!" A beguiling woman of Teutonic legend who, after revealing the secret of how to slay her beloved Siegfried, years later summons her no-less-dear brothers, accused of murdering Siegfried, into a mortal trap. This was your cherished model: "After ten years, I suddenly pull the chair out!" These were your precise words. But all these chairs you jerked out, sometimes without even waiting, echoing the endless lament of abandonment—Ines with Luigi, Claudia with her magician, Gilles with the firms wanting him, Victoire with Dior, let's not talk about Laure who abandoned you for a Christmas Eve—all these trapdoors you opened, sometimes with a bang, did they make you happier?

One step outside of your world, and you pull the chair out instantly, screaming treason right and left. All the chairs you piled up must have created completely useless heaps. But that was precisely part of your nature: you collected "friends" and could not bear it if they lived another life outside of yours, like a child who wants to keep all his toys close by.

⁂

VICTIMS AND MUSES

You spread horrors to justify your rejection of people who no longer suited you. Anna, your most faithful muse, who for so many years had helped nourish your inspiration in a constant quest for renewal, was a blemish on the conventional décor of Monaco parties. She was too shocking, too eccentric and unglamorous for the wealthy, sanitized world of the Riviera. One day you said to me, "Anna, it's time she changed her look. At her age she should stop playing the ridiculous doll, she should dress soberly in navy blue." She embarrassed you, and you pretended that she hadn't returned a book so you would feel justified getting rid of her. At that time, you were a bit full figured and dressed in black to hide your curves. Later, much older yourself, you ended up turning into a walking doll, forgetting the good advice you had wanted to give to others.

Ines de la Fressange was a revelation when she arrived on the catwalks, those springboards to fashion stardom. Long-limbed and clever, a flat-chested beauty contrasting with your Schlemmerian ideals. But on a trip you took to America, a plastic surgeon scientifically analyzed the incredible perfection of your new muse's facial bones. You came back and told me with astonishment that there was no face in the world more remarkable than hers. But nature had also endowed her with a somewhat gangly carriage and an ever-alert intelligence. The whole thing worked wonders and even brought flexibility to the old Coco Chanel suit. Years of success and the impertinence of the muse who actually advised you on creations ended up wearying you. When a handsome Italian appeared in her life and she wanted to marry him, it was too much for you. Luigi dared to snub you, and the project to remodel the national heroine Marianne in Ines's image was the pretext for her final repudiation. Ines also had ideas about fashion and she ended up creating her own line of clothing, with windows and a storefront on Avenue Montaigne. You criticized everything from the start, only later to make up with her.

You had a lot of ideas, but you didn't like it when others borrowed them. "Who created? It is me, not her." You repeated this regularly, and your quarrels with Andrée Putman were recurrent. You wrote about her to me one day: "She has become insufferable, her organization slows everything down, and for money, it borders on the criminal, especially when it comes to interpreting my ideas!" You were obviously putting too much pressure on dear Andrée, who knew perfectly well how to assist you in the numerous arrangements of space for your houses, or your studios, like that of Chanel. When she died, you sent two large black-and-white compositions to frame her coffin, which made people think that it was you inside.

Money often leads to quarrels: someone had given you some that you could not return, someone else needed some, and you did not take care of it, the result being that two grandes dames of French cinema, whom you had earlier spoken of as exceptional women, fell out of grace with you. Stéphane

Audran, whom you had dressed many times—once for Babette's Feast—*did not want to see you again. As for Anouk Aimée, quite dear to Jacques and whom you dressed for* The General of the Dead Army, *with Mastroianni, you described her then as the most magical woman on the planet. But you kicked her out of your world as well.*

For the blonde Claudia Schiffer, the fashion version of Bardot, when you realized that she was becoming more famous than you, you had not yet invented your doll, and when she let herself be seduced by a magician you declared she was out of fashion. Laure was right, quarreling was indeed one of your annoying tendencies. But women were not the only ones to suffer your sudden anger after a fleeting period of benevolence. After years at your side, one day Gilles found a note from you on his desk, where all you had written was the name of a brand that wanted to contact him; it was all spying and jealousy. When he later quit Chanel to work at Balmain (a funny thing, since that's where you started), you didn't even say goodbye. One day a journalist told you he was standing right behind you; you didn't even turn your head.

Your relations with people sometimes bounced back and forth like a ping-pong ball: I love you, I love you not. One of your favorite teammates in this sport was André Leon Talley, the big guy, master of fashion talk. His impressive size, uncommon personality, and deadly laugh made him an immeasurable monument to this frivolous world. Once I even convinced him to come skating with me at Rockefeller Center. The New Yorkers who passed by that day were very impressed. With Jacques he had discovered that decadence was an intellectual and worldly attitude of the highest importance. André always loved to write. A woman once told him, "You love words" and the letters you two exchanged ended up being a great literary correspondence. The most famous interjection in your letters was when André, riding on his own remarks about life, signed his letter "City Light" and you replied bluntly "Black Out."

⁂

THE PHOTOGRAPHER

"Why does Karl make such shitty pictures?" The man who sentenced him without appeal was a well-known and much admired person in the art world. His probity, his honesty, and the fact that he liked Karl very much, and that the feeling was mutual, banished any aggressive connotations from these words. Marc Blondeau was not looking at me when he asked the question. We were in an airplane, he was lost in thought, not accusations. I took a moment to answer, a bit surprised by his words. An image flashed through my mind, a museum (Beaubourg, why not?), with the photos of Nan Goldin, Cindy Sherman, Sebastião Salgado, Guy Bourdin, and perhaps also Ren Hang on the walls. And Karl. No, unfortunately, he could not compare with the others. But why then? I explained to Marc the undeniable technical qualities of Karl's photographs, his quest for perfection, and the culture to which he was so attached. Karl had books on all the great photographers and rightly said, "Guy Bourdin reinvented color in photography after Man Ray." Yes, it was all true, but the basic problem remained. I finally recognized that Karl could not let go of anything, couldn't spit it out. He remained fixed in his convictions and his viewpoints, unlike the process of artistic creation, which requires the artist to speak the truth, starting with his own. I had done artistic direction for *Vogue Paris*, I had worked with the greatest, but strangely enough, every time I went to see Karl the photographer, I never really looked at his work. There were a good dozen young people, all enthusiastic, involved, all diligently carrying out the various tasks at the studio, all unconditionally devoted to his talent. I encouraged him but could not help him. Karl made "pretty photos." In the preface of his first book of photographs, he wrote: "A photographer like me is more of an image maker, or a kind of stage director."

Busy and keen on the perfect progress of the session, I saw him happy, and that was the most important thing. One thing I remember: he had begun doing some camerawork himself with the help of the faithful Éric Pfrunder, under the pretext that the Chanel press campaigns were not up to scratch. This was already a bad excuse. But what was different was that he had ceased his solitary drawing. It had been a long time since he had sketched Anna Piaggi, his former muse, so the new passion replaced the old one. Jacques was already quite ill when he began doing photographs. Karl hoped, without really believing, that he could be treated, and perhaps saved. His studio was a happy hive of activity where he was able to forget everything, which helped him get through the day.

It was probably much better this way. Amidst this whirlwind of assistants, a young woman with a slim figure, lively gestures, very short hair, and a smile, attended to the master's every wish. Caroline Lebar posed for Karl while supervising the interminable sessions that ran on into the night. Karl had rightly written, "I would be lost without my team."

And then, doing photography also means having a different gaze on the world, and Karl could play with that and build his fashion, or rather his styles, still more freely. One day, for fun, he made a corset from a collage of Polaroid photos.

EDWARD STEICHEN
I will never forget the day when we were both in the middle of setting up the Villa Jako in Hamburg, looking for graphics to hang on the walls of a bathroom. You took a photograph out of a box and said, "I love this one! Look, it's Steichen, a few trees, a bit of water, the moon, and solitude." It was my first view of The Pond—Moonlight, *which MoMA would later buy back at a high price. You shared this thought with Pépita: "Photography is the only tangible trace of the ephemeral. It is its fragile and melancholic power that attracts me." That photo made a profound impression on me and would later greatly inspire my work. Thank you, dear Karl, for this discovery.*

⁂

"HE HATED TO BE CALLED AN ARTIST"

In her tribute to Karl at his funeral, Lady de Wintour pronounced what she intended to be fateful words. Of course, in the eyes of his admirers, Karl's genius could only be likened to that of an artist, but this was not how the artist in question looked at it. Karl had a very particular relationship with art. The fact that he remembered the sentence from his childhood—and may even have agreed with it—that he was destined for fashion, not art, was reason enough not to compare himself to artists that he encountered over the course of his life. But when Jacques was spending time in Francis Bacon's studio on Rue de Birague talking and drinking, Karl preferred to keep out of it, and never bought a work by the master. When Andy Warhol was in Paris, he and Karl saw a lot of each other. But there again, there was no purchase or even a portrait

"I will have the château razed to the ground and ask Tadao to build me a contemporary home with all the functions I need."

commission for the star of Pop. He eventually acquired a drawing by Hockney because it was of Jacques. No question, Karl was perfectly clear about the value of an artist, but he kept his distance from their art. He felt more at ease with the old masters, as exemplified in our collection of seventeenth- and eighteenth-century French paintings. He could not collect contemporary artists. Perhaps the repressed artist in him shied away from any comparison. "Never compare, never compete" was his motto.

Karl was a master in the art of plagiarism, and knew how to find a relevant interpretation of a style, whether in fashion or art. In one of his Chanel show installations he brilliantly displayed his talent by replicating at the Grand Palais a typical contemporary art gallery in gray cement. He filled it with intellectual concrete: no fewer than seventy-five prints recalling the works of prominent artists of the time. All these "in the manner of" in their humorous setting must have brought a smile to connoisseurs—artists perhaps less. Most of them never learned they had been "part of the joke," so distant were the orbits of art and fashion.

It must be said that Karl judged an artist as a man without any consideration for his fame. We were in our first arrangement in the Hôtel Pozzo when he organized a dinner for Jeff Koons. At the time the artist was living with La Cicciolina, the provocative sex icon and the source of his creativity. At the end of the evening, Karl said, "The real whore of the two is not the one you think." Later, when he was thinking of creating a mobile art museum, with Zaha Hadid as architect, he left the task of selecting the artists to the art critic Fabrice Bousteau. But even more than artists, he truly admired architects; he was more excited about Zaha than about the selected artists. The architect who most aroused his passion was unquestionably Tadao Ando. The adventure with the famous Japanese architect began much earlier. Karl invited us to the inauguration of the Meditation Space he had built for the UNESCO headquarters in Paris. It was not very large but intelligently conceived and soberly presented, like all Ando's creations. Karl was intrigued by the use of light. A few days later, he called me because he had just been proposed a piece of land in a French forest with a turn-of-the-century neo-Renaissance château, a perfect caricature of the provincial prefecture. "I will have the château razed to the ground and ask Tadao to build me a contemporary home with all the functions I need," he said. I encouraged him, but the project fell through some time later. Karl had received a letter from the local prefecture, forbidding him to touch the château and local ecologists also gave him quite a tongue-lashing, panicking at the idea that he might cut down some trees to realize his project. Karl said to me furiously, "That's not the way to save their forest." But he was not finished with Tadao and when he moved to Biarritz he again wanted him to intervene alongside the Basque house. Showing me a long furrow in the ground he said, "See, there, I can clearly see a long wing facing north. I am going to talk to Tadao about it. I will put my studio and library there; it will be my new life." But that would not happen: the wing was built, but not with the same talent. Karl claimed that the mayor of Biarritz had rejected Tadao's beautiful project but the truth is that it was a simple and unfortunate lack of funds.

Artist, architect, Karl was none of these things, but he dreamed continuously and, with him, dreams often came true. He wrote: "As a child, before I discovered fashion, I dreamed of being a portraitist or a director."

The question remains, unanswered: what could Karl have done if he had not been a fashion designer? An artist? A writer? Perhaps even a producer? He was rarely wrong in his perception of others. He picked up the qualities and faults of his fellow men at the speed of light. As for himself, his attempts to escape the label of "fashion designer" were evident in the plethora of photographs he took and his many albums on photography. Other experiments proved less successful, such as his recent foray into sculpture, miniature architectures revisited. But twice, and without realizing it himself, he created some true works of art that were not clothing, and they deserve to be recognized as such.

⁂

SUFFER AND CREATE

Your favorite realm was drawing. You excelled at it; every year you made hundreds of sketches for your work. Some of them were very fleeting, barely sketched and soon thrown in the wastebasket, but they were enough to show the seamstress an effect you sought or a detail you wanted to change. Your hand glided over the paper, it seemed to barely graze it. Your gesture was guided by an idea, always precise, never uncertain. Vincent recalls that you started by drawing an eye on paper and the whole character would follow. The person, her character, her attitude dominated the question of what clothes would dress the silhouette. The precious book you wrote with Anna, a collection of years of your drawings of her clothing inventions, perfectly expresses this value you cherished. If Antonio, whom you admired, favored the silhouette over the individual, you did exactly the opposite.

But one work, unique and known only to a few, deserves being rediscovered and interpreted more carefully. Jacques was dying, his hours were numbered. We were in Le Mée, not far away. The house was radiant, the sky blue—of course the days would be happy while you suffered. You hid it, of course, and wanted to laugh and make us laugh. One afternoon, you asked me to help you take a table and a chair into the garden. You placed it not far from the house. You brought your pencils, your pastels, your gouaches, and a profusion of drawing paper and announced to me, "I am going to make an illustrated book. I have an idea in mind. You know the story of the Emperor's New Clothes?" You set to work straightaway and for days and days I watched you playing with black ink and the brightest colors. Some time earlier, I had asked you to do the illustrations in Vogue *for a series written by Alexandre Pradère, "The Metamorphoses of Madame Haugoult-Dujour," inspired by Philippe Jullian. At the time I found your drawings too heavily contoured in black but I didn't say anything. When the new work was finished, you had it published in Germany under the title* Des Kaisers, Neue Kleider. *You gave me a copy, which I passed on to one of your American admirers without thinking. I have only recently managed to recover this masterpiece. In my opinion it is a remarkable work you have accomplished here.*

We recognize all your sources of graphic inspiration; one thinks of the expressionists and their emphasized and dramatic black contours—Kirchner, Pechstein, or Schmidt-Rottluff. As for colors, we see Jawlensky's faces made-up in multicolored patches. I believe you adored him above all else. But here drama mixed with caricature, the emperor becomes a strange, funny, and at times sad Louis XIV. His palace looks like Versailles while the city is totally Germanic and festive. We recognize your passion for the early naïve paintings of Kandinsky. In one of the drawings we also find an allusion to Aubrey Beardsley. As for the layout, it is remarkable and you also designed, with intelligence and humor, the box that contains the book. It is not a book for children, but a work of art that adults can appreciate, and a veritable treasure for bibliophiles.

I remember furtive moments when your sadness appeared, in spite of your desire to chase it away. That suffering has undoubtedly allowed you to open the depths of your nature. Trauma is also a source of revelation for the artist.

⁂

THE INSTALLATIONS IN THE GRAND PALAIS

"When a man is old he must do more than when he was young."

— GOETHE

You, who loved to quote Goethe, heeded well this dictum. But you were very young when you got the idea of creating a background for a fashion show. It was for Chloé. We had just installed some pretty trellises in the courtyard at Grand-Champ and so, the following year, you designed a set with a trellis to present the Chloé summer collection. After that, décor became inseparable from the concept of your collections. And when you finally achieved glory and the exceptional resources of Chanel, you gave your imagination free rein, free also from the straightjacket of clothing. At that point you created not sets, but installations. There was no connection between an interstellar rocket and a tweed tailleur, however modern it might be, but the installation was remarkable in its short life. The general public had little or no access to the creations you realized for Chanel. Only the guests, the fashion business professionals, and a few friends, all caring, most of all, about the collection, had this privilege, without really understanding the value of these installations. The living forest, the sublime trees, the endless beach, the planted wheat, the Fellinian cruise ship, the supermarket temple of consumerism... there were so many inventions in the installations you created in step with the seasonal cycles of fashion. No, they were not scenery, they were installations. When Olafur Eliasson put hunks of glacial ice in front of the Panthéon in Paris for his Ice Watch *as a warning about global warming, no journalist recalled your enormous iceberg melting symbolically under the glass dome of the Grand Palais. It is true, of course, that they are not the same journalists: some talk about art, others about fashion.*

Your installations in the majestic pavilion of the great universal exhibitions in Paris deserve recognition worthy of the artist that you did not know you were.

⁂

November 25, 1954, the first Lagerfeld-Saint Laurent challenge. They both won first prize, but not as equals. Karl would later get his revenge by taking over the studio of Gabrielle Chanel.

Top: Karl's auction at Christie's in Monte Carlo in 2000.
Above: Pierre Bergé and Yves Saint Laurent's sale at the Grand Palais in 2009. This time, Yves and Pierre were the victors, more than doubling the amount of Karl's sale.

Installation for the eyes of the fashion world only, under the dome of the Grand Palais in Paris. A rocket takes off to inaugurate the Chanel show—a magnificent demonstration of Karl's inventive spirit.

ANEL
17/18
PAR
GABRIELLE CHANEL · AGENCE SPATIALE

Photograph, photograph, and photograph again. Photo as an art of living, or surviving, fleeing the story told by time and recreating everything in the present.

Galignani! The name of this historic Paris bookstore evokes the passion that accompanied Karl through a life of tireless book browsing.

RUINED

Ever since he was a child, Karl had always been very easy with money. His father gave it to him, lubricating his move to Paris and comfortable, affluent lifestyle there. But, of course, he quickly began working and his income rose steadily. Karl's fortune derived exclusively from his work. Everything went swimmingly for the young designer over the years. His mind adapted to creative diversity and learned to develop multiple unrelated collections simultaneously. His motto in this regard was simple and to the point: "No money, no ideas." When he was finally taken on by Chanel, he became a grand bourgeois and saw himself as a businessman. He had gone from airliner—first class, naturally—to private jet with free boarding at Le Bourget.

But the fortune-teller—the dear Madame Serakian, who had accurately predicted a radiant future for Karl and had even pointed out to him, without having read it, that on page 7 of the contract he was about to sign with Chanel there was a clause that would cause him pain—should have warned him that beautiful La Vigie was a trap, located on French soil and not in Monaco as he had believed. This villa was not going to bring him luck. One day, after having invested a fortune in this Trianon of the Riviera, he found a squadron of stern-faced men in gray at his door in Paris, claiming to be from the Palais de Bercy; not from the lovely château which is no more, but from the French Ministry of Finance. It was the beginning of a long, agonizing, and impoverishing descent. We were in the green room of the Hôtel Pozzo when I saw Lucien—Monsieur Frydlender, the chargé d'affaires—arrive looking very worried, preceding the birds of ill omen. A small, grizzled man who was cheerful as a rule, that day Lucien was red, spoke in bursts, rolled his eyes, and fidgeted left and right. Karl asked me to leave the house immediately. I exited through the kitchen and saw the ugly vultures arrive in the courtyard. "You live in La Vigie and so you have to pay your taxes to France," they told him.

Thus began his ordeal. At the time we were spending a lot of money. We bought furniture and paintings at auctions and from galleries and were doing work at each of the houses. Karl did not keep track of money and I even less, to the point where he later said, "With Patrick, I had the impression that he was the rich one." But that day, La Vigie was his ruin. He never admitted his weaknesses. I never heard a word of any difficulties. He certainly received help in this misfortune, but he was never able to achieve the same splendor he once knew. He was able to maintain his lifestyle and legendary generosity, continuing to give flowers and gifts to his friends, but money was tight. He wanted to help Olivier de Rohan, who had just taken over the apartments vacated by Gérald Van der Kemp at Versailles. Olivier was then president of the Friends of Versailles association and hoped Karl would be among the donors. We were on the spot and Karl kept saying to me, "You need to give them some ideas to arrange all that." Karl was very good at sending me out in front to take care of this type of situation. I got to work with Olivier, who was very happy for the help, but it was only recently that he confided that Karl had never given him a cent. This surprised me because I had always seen Karl contributing to many cultural and scientific foundations, especially during Jacques's illness. Why hadn't he given anything here? Did he think, like many philanthropists, that Versailles was rich and had no need for his money? More simply, he thought he was running out of money, but he could not say it. It never crossed his lips with me; he attributed all the moves that followed to new and fleeting desires.

Hoping to save his neck from the taxman, he thought that getting rid of La Vigie without delay would be a good move. So he had all the furniture removed from this ill-fated Trianon, a good portion of which was moved back to Villa Jako. However, the financial disaster forced him in the end to sell Grand-Champ, Le Mée, and, finally, Villa Jako. He was driven back to the favorable Monegasque territory, to Monte Carlo, to a very ugly apartment furnished with furniture from the 1940s that couldn't have been any more conventional. Large windows overlooked the flat sea and the boring view of this failed Rothko was only occasionally enlivened by a large ship on the horizon.

His depression only got worse, and he kept gaining weight.

⁂

ELISABETH'S ASHES

The vacation was over and we had not spent much time at Grand-Champ. Jacques was at war with Rafael, the château caretaker, and hardly came there anymore. Meanwhile Karl was busy with his next collection. One afternoon he called us and asked us to join him at Chloé as quickly as possible. Jacques and I arrived together and went to the desk where Karl was drawing. He looked at us, flashed a little embarrassed smile and said, "My mother has just died. There will be no ceremony; she did not want one. And we won't go there. Her ashes will be scattered in the park according to her wishes."

Later, strolling along the beautiful allée in the park at Grand-Champ, I thought of her and imagined she was watching us go by. It was just the two of us, Karl and me, for most of these strolls. At the end of the grand allée I had had a statue of Hercules put up, resting on his club. We kept talking. At the end of the lane we walked into the forest glade, filled with delightfully fragrant wild hyacinths. Karl called this part of the estate "Perfumer's Corner." We made our way through the undergrowth down to the path leading back to the château. It ran along a small, placid brook, the Loc. Gazing at the bucolic watercourse, Karl would always allude to the battle of the Loc bridge, an episode from the Chouannerie in the final years of the Revolution: "Seeing it like this, it is hard to imagine a great Revolutionary battle." The bridge was quite small and couldn't have been more romantic. He would add, "At the time, this stream must have been much wider." I pointed out the relatively flat terrain on the other side of the stream, which must have been swampy at the time. We never mentioned Elisabeth. She was there but all we talked about was our grand project. Rafael and his wife Pilar had taken up residence in her apartments as best they could while waiting for the château to be enlarged and furnished. Karl readily admitted that they certainly deserved a comfortable lodging in the house. I stayed out of that part of it. Rafael and I did a phenomenal reconstruction of the gardens. We dynamited the ground where necessary, planted lindens, enlarged the main entrance to the estate, built a stone orangery with fully copper plumbing, and created new pools. I bought stone benches and urns and old sculptures to decorate the large pool that had replaced the sloping orchard on the west side of the château. The peacock pigeons had all disappeared but the estate was magnificent.

Elisabeth was gone; Jacques didn't come anymore. We dreamed of an ideal house, one that Voltaire would have liked. At the Hôtel Pozzo in Paris the

"The ashes, he doesn't deserve them, they will stay with me!"

collection of paintings and furniture continued to grow. It was a most prestigious furniture storehouse, with treasures destined for a Breton manor.

Then, years later, the strangest story of our relationship took place. It had to do with Karl's mother. Jacques was dead and the money was running out. To my surprise, Karl called me one afternoon. He was working in the Chanel studio and didn't want to be heard. He was very worked up and spoke in a hush. "You go to Grand-Champ. I can no longer set foot there because Rafael has become insufferable, and I also have too much work. Lucien will write you a letter and you can collect my mother's ashes." I was stunned, so surprised that I couldn't think. But discretion was obviously required. I answered that of course I would do what he asked and told no one about it. I was both flattered that he had asked me to do this precious errand and shocked to find out her ashes were still in their urn. Armed with Lucien's letter, which gave me authority over said ashes, I called the château. Pilar had died several years earlier and Rafael was living alone. He was not surprised by my call and was rather curt over the phone. I traveled in splendid weather, a real Atlantic sky, and didn't dwell on things—what would have been the point? Rafael was waiting for me at Vannes station, which had hardly changed in all these years. He didn't say a word. I got into the car and commented on the fair weather, while he responded in monosyllables, concentrating on his driving. After arriving at the house, he marched ahead of me like a colonel; I didn't even want to look at the gardens, much less the rooms. We entered the large kitchen. The oxblood-red and white tiles were coming loose and clattered under our feet. At the center of the long table I saw only two place settings, for him and me, face to face. I talked about the house, complimenting him on how well he was keeping everything. Of course there was no serving staff. He had prepared our plates with the local charcuterie. There was bread and butter, not to mention wine. I was hungry and didn't hold back, happy to have something to engage in, because the conversation was strained. He eventually said that I was kind and his voice soon began to break. The proud Spaniard was surrendering and I did my best to comfort him. Suddenly, looking at me with tears in his eyes, he began to cry out, "Monsieur, do you know what? He didn't do anything. Pilar and I took care of his mother. He didn't even come to visit her. We loved and cared for her until she died. He didn't even give us money, and I'll tell you." I no longer focused on the tears wetting his wrinkled skin, I saw his eyes darkening with rage. "The ashes, he doesn't deserve them, they will stay with me!" Taken aback by this sudden vehemence, at first I didn't know how to answer, but somehow I found words. I felt sorry for him, but I did not want to listen to those accusations. All I could think about was taking Elisabeth's ashes to Paris and giving them to Karl. In the end I said to him, "Rafael, I beg you! She is not your mother and she is not mine, we're talking about Karl's mother. Every child has a right to have his mother with him. You cannot take his away. I understand all your grievances, and I understand your bitterness. I see what you have endured, but neither you nor I can forbid him from taking back what belongs to him by nature."

After a bit more crying and shouting, he calmed down. "Okay," he said, "but you are going to sign a paper for me." He looked around and found a sheet of paper. I took a pencil and wrote that I, the undersigned, was taking back the ashes of Madame Lagerfeld from Rafael Roubio, discharging him of his duty on this spring day, etc.

But we were not done yet. I could not wait to take the precious package in hand and had only one thought in my head: not to miss my train. He asked me to follow him. We walked through the château and arrived in what had once been Elisabeth's room. Rafael had now made it his own. An atmosphere of fatigue and dissolution had invaded this once cheerful place. Next to the window, the sofa with the lacquered frame, the one used in Guy Bourdin's pretty picture in the old orchard, now looked sad and dirty. Rafael went around behind it, squatted down and brought out an old, half-opened grocery box. In it was an urn covered with a greenish patina, like antique bronze. He took it in his arms, hugged it close and started crying again. With mounting emotion he wailed, "No! No!" I went over and tried to take the urn from him. He held it close, while I pulled it toward me saying, "Come on Rafael, you have suffered enough, let him have it." He didn't want to hear it. We were each tugging at the poor urn, which I was afraid would break, scattering Elisabeth all over the room. Finally, I managed to pull the urn away from him. He was devastated.

On the way back, I told him he had to start another life, far away in Spain, amidst his beloved orange orchard that he knew how to tend so well. I felt relieved on the train and I did not try to understand Karl's lie about the ashes—his own mother's ashes—which he told us had been spread in the park. I kept the box next to me and did not open it until I got home. It was only then that I realized that the urn was made of plastic. I called Karl immediately but did not mention this unexpected detail to him. He thanked me, asking "It wasn't too hard?" I said nothing about the theatrical scene earlier at the château and asked what he wanted me to do. "You know what we are going to do? We will go to Goyard and order a suitcase with two compartments, one for my mother, the other for Jacques." Without even thinking, I answered, "Excellent idea. But what should I do with the urn in the meantime?" He responded matter-of-factly, "You will keep it at home until then."

The events of that day had disturbed me quite a bit and I did not have the head to go on thinking about it. I didn't want to think about the ashes not being scattered in the park. My only concern was to find a place for them out of reach of the housekeeper. The bookcase in my bedroom was perfect for that. Placed on a high shelf where it would be seen from below, the urn would be mistaken for an antique vase. So I went to bed every night wishing Elisabeth well.

That went on for two years, but I've always gotten on well with ghosts.

⁂

WORDS AND LAUGHTER

Named after its inventor, the Almanach Vermot *is an old French tradition, a veritable bible of jokes and puns which has been published every year for over a century. Each day of the year has a funny story to help us find the lighter side of life. Dear Karl, you, too, filled every day with your witticisms and clever jokes and laughed at other people's jokes as much as your own. You could have published your own almanac, a Diary of Laughter. Indeed, some of your bons mots are famous and were even published; others are frequent refrains. Some were a bit risqué and perhaps a bit over the top in this age of political correctness.*

"Sex, most of the time, we sit on it." You liked to say this, especially in response to overly intimate questions. You were taking a famous phrase by Michel de Montaigne and turning it around: "On the world's highest throne, our seat is still our bottom." We might restate it: no matter how lofty your seat, you are still sitting on your ass.

Among spirited jokes about sex, you always loved one—very British and outmoded—of a young nobleman with "unnatural" tendencies. His parents sought to instruct him by enlisting the services of an experienced madam. While their son and she retired, the impatient parents pressed their ears to the door, hearing the lady cry out, "No, no! Not there! There!"

On the subject of women, your borrowed your favorite phrase from the misogynist Paul Léautaud, who only wrote about what pleased him. When asked to define a good woman, he replied "A woman who is not good."

But you preferred to laugh at anecdotes of everyday life, sometimes colorful, sometimes over the top. We were leaving for Brittany and did not have our own driver to take us to the station. In the taxi on the way, you realized that you had to get cash from an ATM and so we stopped. When you came back you were laughing so hard I thought you would choke. A couple were ahead of you at the ATM. The man, unable to get his card to work, became increasingly angry, shouting at the machine as he tried in vain to get his card into the slot. "Swallow it!" he cried. Without missing a beat, the woman responded, "Sounds like you're talking to me."

There were times, of course, when you could not help being a little impolite, anything but politically correct. One day a charming little lady on the street approached you with a collection box, thinking that a well-dressed gentleman like yourself would be certain to show generosity to her cause: "It is for teenage mothers."

You did not hesitate, "Ah no! They've had their fun, we're not going to pay for it!" The lady was absolutely crushed. A little embarrassed, you slipped a bill into her collection box, but you could not help chuckling, delighted with your provocation.

Laughter was daily fare with you and there were no complaints. Your ability to laugh and make others laugh is all the more remarkable given that your own life had not been happy. You advocated the optimism of the German woman, who, celebrating her hundredth birthday, gave you the secret to what kept her going: "I want to know what is going to happen tomorrow." You were ecstatic and translated for me. Curiosity is, indeed, what it's all about—discovering things and being passionate about them, it's all there.

⌘

AUTOMOBILES

While Karl blew kisses to the mayor of Paris, high priestess of the city of scooters, he never stopped being driven by car. And he liked them big, from the longest Rolls to the widest Hummer.

One day, Brahim had left the car in the courtyard of the Hôtel Pozzo. We had decided to go to a restaurant and, of course, there was absolutely no thought of walking there. "I know how to drive, actually," said Karl. "I should be able to get us there." Excited about the adventure, with me confident and amused, we got into the vehicle. He carefully surveyed all the controls on the dashboard, as if it were an airplane. Then he turned the ignition and the engine purred to life. I don't know exactly what happened next but the car lurched ahead, then again—forward, yes, but not in the right direction. I said to him, "Take your time, you'll make it." He restarted the motor and miraculously we inched along, very slowly. But the motor stalled again and we came to a stop. "Ah, these cars are too sophisticated!" he said. "Things were simple when I was driving my Beetle. Now it's all complicated." The solution was simple. We left the car crosswise in the courtyard and hailed a cab.

While Karl's driving left something to be desired, Jacques was an expert. He glided over the roads in a fluid and comfortable flow. He also had a passion for beautiful old cars. Of course, when he met Karl he only had a 2CV and Karl, no snob, happily climbed in. But Jacques could see himself driving a Duesenberg and he also liked to drive Jeeps. In the summer we would set out from the château with a picnic basket, I in front with Jacques, Anna Piaggi in the back seat, a Manganesque vision, or Visconti, in her hat and veil, turning the heads of the locals, unaccustomed to such pageantry. We left Karl to work at the château and headed for the beach. What beautiful days those were!

Being chauffeur driven all those years, I never saw the great use in learning how to drive, but then one day on Rue Rivoli I looked at the faces of the drivers lined up at a traffic light. If they could drive, I could drive. Without telling anyone, I started taking lessons and soon got my license. My mother had an old car that she no longer used and I invited Karl for a drive. He was flabbergasted and complimented my driving, but on the Cours la Reine the motor stopped. It was hell getting it started again. It was Karl who offered me my first car—I was a spoiled child.

"Things were simple when I was driving my Beetle. Now it's all complicated."

Some friends of ours were getting married one day in a small village in Provence. Karl lent me the Bentley that Bernard, the nice Monegasque driver, drove, very chauffeur-like. It caused quite a stir in the village!

For Karl, the car was the most pleasant way to get around, provided it was spacious and very comfortable with a high roof.

⁂

Except for the Beetle he drove during his youth, and my first car, I never saw Karl in a small car. He had his Rolls early on, a Bentley later. They were modern-day carriages to him.

77 LU75

GLORY AND GLOOM 1990–

Les Fils Invisibles *(Invisible Threads), a photo from my collection* Nuit, le pouvoir de l'obscur *(Night, The Power of Darkness), evokes our encounters and passage through life.*

Elisabeth and Jacques were gone forever, Karl, laureled with honors, was well into his autumn years. The crowds adored him, but deep inside he was alone.

Franck Laigneau, the pretext for the rupture. Karl was jealous, no doubt, but in love with me? I would not go that far.

FRANCK

Victoire de Castellane got married at Les Invalides with a crowd of fashion's upper crust gathered at the historic military monument. Shortly before, I had made the acquaintance of Franck Laigneau, an amazing young man, as intelligent as he was radiant. Like Karl and Louis XIV, he was a Virgo, and like them, there was something of the sun about him. He hated being left in the background and kept pestering me to introduce him to Karl. I had brought a Polaroid camera to the wedding, which Franck came and took; I had no idea what he was going to do with it. When he came back, he said, teasing and triumphant, "I saw Karl!" I still didn't know what he had done but it turned out to be fully worthy of his bravado: camera in hand, he had gone in search of Karl, planted himself in front of him, and taken a photo. He then gave the Polaroid to Karl, telling him "It's from Patrick!" That was all it took to provoke the cataclysm. Not knowing Franck, Karl would have asked his entourage who he was and immediately imagined that the bold youngster was a friend of mine—I had never before introduced any friend of mine to him. Karl did not say anything to me, but the die was cast: it would take him years to get away from me.

Franck later became a well-known gallery owner in Paris. He specialized in turn-of-the-century Baltic vernacular art, which gained him a certain renown among museums. He had a rather intellectual clientele, Bob Wilson among them. Karl had to find out about this talented young man and, feigning a lack of interest, he spied on his boutique to assess Franck's originality. One day, he discreetly bought a Harry Napper chair from him. Karl recognized intelligence when he saw it.

⁂

THE ASHES RETURN

Jacques was dead; Elisabeth slept chez moi.

Days followed nights, the weeks passed, months too. You said you were increasingly absorbed in your work but it was clear that you were seeking distance from me. You wrote me long letters mentioning all sorts of people who, from your point of view, had behaved dishonestly with you, leading me to observe that "those people" were also my friends. And I noted that they had also been yours. Your letters became more and more aggressive. The people in question were all renowned authorities in art, scholars and dealers, without forgetting the one you were most angry with, Laure. One of them escaped your criticism, but history always reaches its own inexorable conclusions, because the only one, according to you, who hadn't robbed you has now ended up in prison. Strangely, you never stated the real reason for your jealousy, Franck, but you did sling a lot of mud in the letters you sent me. You once even used the word "ordure" [excrement/bastard], a word I had never heard cross your lips, much less seen in writing, and always closed your letters with "Je t'embrasse" [I kiss you]. Money was at the heart of your worries, but hiding it from others was an absolute rule for you. I couldn't talk to anyone about it. I was confused and didn't know what to think. I visited you from time to time during those famous photo shoots, but you appeared to be absorbed in your work and kept your back turned to me, barely saying a word. Once or twice, you wanted to show me a new installation for your new domain on Rue de Lille. Then you would brighten, ask my advice, and seek my approval.

For two years Elisabeth had been sleeping in my room. Finally one day—and I am grateful for that day—you sent me this note:

"Dear Patrick,

Please bring me my mother's things. Wrap them up as a gift so the servants won't get any ideas about opening the package.

Je t'embrasse,

Karl"

With mounting fury, I reread these lines. The only "thing" I had of your mother was the urn with her ashes. The insinuation about the servants was gratuitous; neither Clément nor Esther would ever have been indiscreet here. Of course, you dismissed them later, they knew too much. I was disgusted.

I went to my craftsmen and ordered a front-opening box with a gilded brass handle and inscribed with the initials E.L. I placed the urn inside, and had the precious boxed sealed shut. When I got home, I wrote you my last letter:

"Karl,
I bring you your mother's ashes, and I will always be sorry that you prefer the lie to the truth.
I wish you all happiness.
Patrick"

I remember standing in front of the mirror, saying, "Karl, you just gave me your best lesson: never do as you do, never cheat myself."

The next day I crossed the empty courtyard of the Hôtel Pozzo, the box in one hand and my letter in the other. I saw the entire Pozzo family coming out. They greeted me happily, we exchanged a few words, and Sandrine could not help asking, "But what do you have there?"

I was evasive, "Karl's things." And then I left for good.

⁂

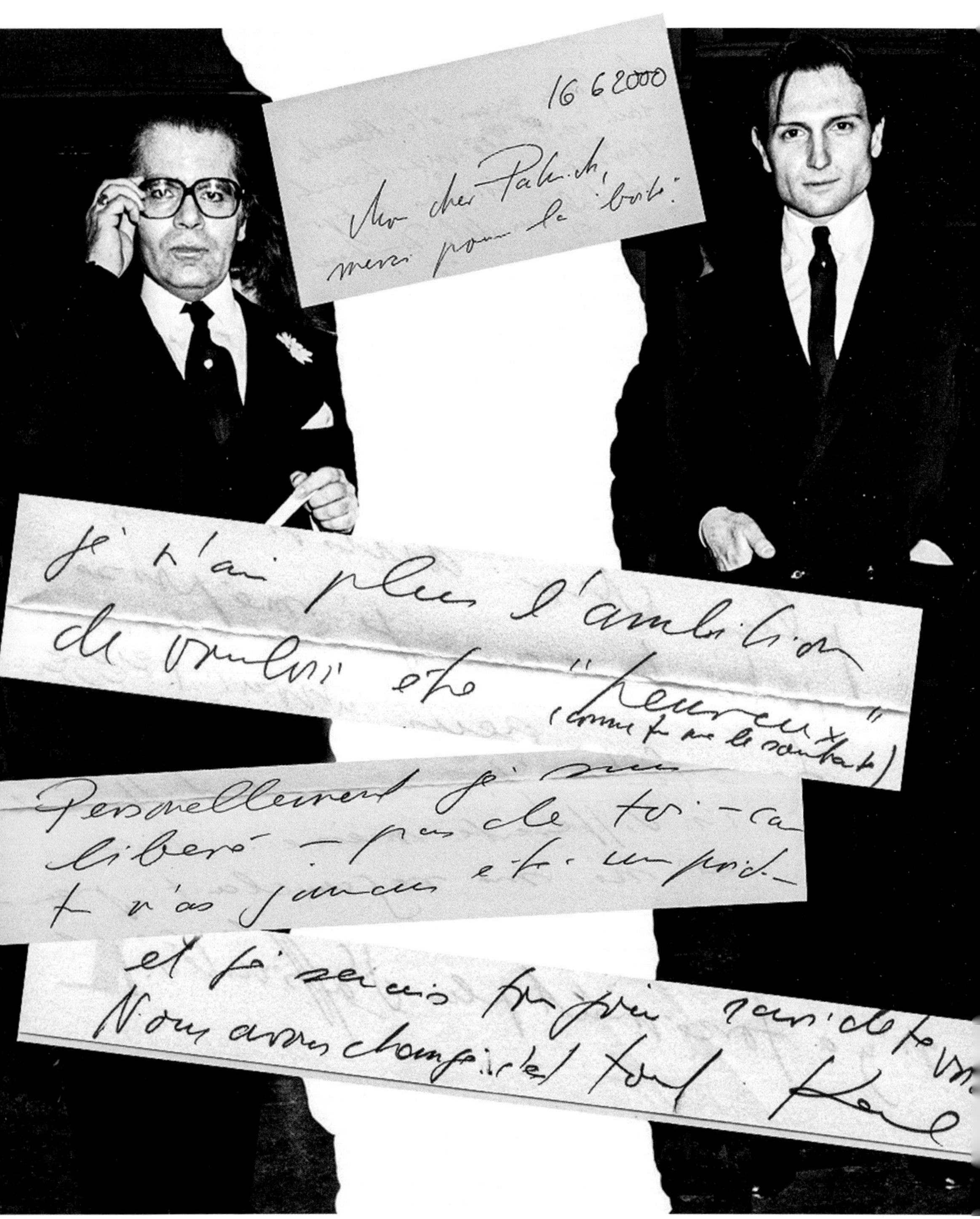

16.6.2000

Mon cher Patrick,
merci pour le "book".

Je n'ai plus l'ambition
de vouloir être "heureux"
(comme tu me le souhaitais)

Personnellement je suis
libéré – pas de toi – ça
tu n'as jamais été un poids –

et je serais toujours ravi de te voir.
Nous avons changé(s) tout. Karl

Your last letter, at the dawn of the new century; the separation was definitive. It was better that way. Je ne regrette rien.[4]

PAGES TORN OUT

You often had multiple copies of the same book, and loved to tear pages from them. This plunder helped you document ideas, create collages, keep a visual trace of everything you discovered by reading. But for you, these torn pages were the image of life itself. Tearing out was the best way for you to move on and forget. You tore out Anna's page, Laure's page, Gilles's, Victoire's, and those of many others. All these missing pages composed your biography and helped you construct your life. But pages torn from life do not fly away, they cannot be destroyed, they will not disappear. You wanted to ignore them, but you could not deny their truth, nor erase their effect.

The letter I wrote to you in my rage against your dressing up of the obvious must have surprised you and cannot have left you unmoved. The morning after the break I had intentionally caused, you wrote me a flood of words, sometimes closely written, sometimes scrawled. You were sweet to me, you said that we had been very happy but also very naïve, even innocent. You said that, bit by bit, "the clouds came"—clouds in the form of others. You used the same thought process as ever: always be right, create your own truth to ensure it, take it to heart, and never go back on it. Thinking back on the entourage you denigrated, you must have thought these people corrupted me. Your paranoia about being forced to sell made it impossible for you to look objectively at people whose integrity has never since been questioned. Today I can better understand your aggressive attitude. Like a wounded man, you hated the whole world for all the misfortunes that you hid from others. But me, you wanted to soothe me. I was wrong to take "such a tragic tone," your "friendship was still intact," and in any case you would "always be happy" to see me. Your letter mourned a bygone time, roads that part. As I reread it, your

---

4. FACING PAGE, TRANSLATED EXCERPTS FROM A PRIVATE LETTER: June 16, 2000. My dear Patrick, thank you for the "box". I no longer have the ambition of wanting to be "happy" (as you want me to be). Personally, I free freed–not from you–as you have never been a weight... and I will always be delighted to see you. We have changed, that's all. — Karl

sense of inescapable destiny became clearer. "I no longer have the ambition to be 'happy' the way you wished," you wrote, certainly believing it. I was saddened to read these words, they sounded like Werther, not like you. We should live and look for what strengthens and elevates us. But you also could not free yourself of grief for your mother. Regarding the ashes that I had returned to you, you could only speak of "the box." It had been a good idea to seal the ugly plastic urn in it—fortunately you never saw it. You said you were free, adding that you didn't mean from me and that I had "never been a burden." But were you really free? It's what you tried to believe, and tried to get your entourage to believe. Pages are to be turned, Karl, not ripped out.

"We have changed, that's all." These were your last words about our story, which was coming to an end with all the fatality of a novel.

Some time later, Nicole Wisniak said to me, "Did you never realize that he loved you?" The question had never occurred to me; if it had I would have felt uncomfortable.

⁂

THE ETERNAL LIE

Dear Karl, you never stopped mocking Françoise Giroud for her I Give You My Word. *You kept saying, "Of course she lies!" But if this woman's lies were justified—starting with survival during the war—yours, frequent and inventive, were much more opportunistic, even pointless. You forgot that you had confided in me in the past, laughing at your exploits, "Every lie, if repeated often enough, becomes the truth." You anticipated today's fake news, but you were getting caught up in your own story.*

Lying can sometimes be a game. Gainsbourg lied happily, but the little fable about your father's Swedish origins, or your mother's aristocratic roots, supposedly related to William II, and a female pilot to boot, were nothing more than little touches of makeup to prettify your life. But other lies had teeth and hurt some people you wanted to get rid of.

The eternal lie became your way of life. You confided to Pépita, "I am very self-preserving; in the end there is little reality to my existence."

You dreamed of a beautiful, intelligent, ideal, and amusing world. You did not like the progress of the planet and society and thus used humor as a weapon against depression, the lie as an antidote to revolution. Denial had become a way of life for you, death only exists if you talk about it, illness is to be avoided. Alas, you had to face Jacques's agony and did not want to go through that again, not even for yourself. When Pierre Hebey became ill, you hastened to stop seeing him, and you acted the same way when Liliane began to fade. You always had to have money, so useful, yet volatile; bankruptcy was only for others. All you had to do was work, and create, continue to move forward and never fall back. And to escape this world, too real in your eyes, you created your own truth; the eternal lie and solitude became your credo. And in solitude one lies only to oneself. Return to solitude, that is precisely what you wrote the day after Jacques's death, "I am made for solitude but I made the mistake of thinking that, with Jacques gone, it would scare me. On the contrary, it is indispensable to me."

⁂

HERITAGE AND VENGEANCE

You liked Gianni Versace a lot. Of course you never talked about fashion with him, but this boy, with his emperor's profile, simple, always smiling, receptive and radiant, could not but please you. Gianni loved houses, grand antiquities—a broad subject of conversation with him for anyone who wanted to jump in. Gianni kept saying that the collection that I "made for you" was a remarkable piece of work, but I always hastened to say that it was together, you and I, that we had acquired all these marvels. If I was the one who found the objects most of the time, it was partly because you did not have the time to spare. You called me every Saturday when we would scan the Gazette de Drouot *together on the phone. Our enthusiasm, our likes and our dislikes were always in harmony. I never presented an object, painting, or sculpture to you that you did not want. In this effort we truly were in perfect tune, perfect "accomplices"; it was rightfully "our collection." But one day you decided to sell the whole thing. In the press you talked about changing times, evolving lifestyles, fashion, when the real reason, hidden but all too true, was the money you owed to the taxman.*

Your quarrel with Laure drove you to entrust the sale to Christie's, which you did not particularly like after the misadventure of Sir Charles Clore's auction in Monte Carlo a few years earlier. A piece of furniture we wanted had come up for sale but we could not be in Monaco so you did the bidding from your pretty yellow room in Paris. I can still see you sitting on a low stool at the foot of your bed. At the time you had a comfortable budget for the piece, but the bidding went beyond it. You hung up and we were in tears, trying to get over it, when the phone rang. To your surprise, it was an employee of Christie's offering the piece at one step up from your highest bid. You always hated schemes and shenanigans and did not understand the reason for this maneuver. "They are trying to cheat me," you told me. You ended up hanging up, exasperated, saying that you would never again do business with those people… But time had passed and you made every effort to get even with Laure.

You had also decided that I should choose a certain number of lots that would be returned to me, a few paintings, a few pieces of furniture. "It will be your inheritance," you said. Thus, I kept the steel bed you had slept in at the Hôtel Pozzo, an austere, Jansenist model which went so well with your taste for Philippe de Champaigne. But what you didn't tell me were the false accusations you made against me among your circle of friends. Pierre Hebey, who knew me well, did not believe you. You then told me that the Hebeys didn't want to see me anymore. Geneviève quickly moved to reassure me and invited Franck and me to Biarritz, which obviously made you furious.

Another time I ran into our friend Liliane's formidable husband, Élie de Rothschild, whose reputation for kindness could not be overstated. He came up to me, his eyes flashing. "I defended you to your former friend. He called you a cheat and a thief. I told him it wasn't true and that he was the liar!" I thanked Elie for this unexpected defense, but I was surprised: I would never have thought of behaving like that with you!

Over the years, we created the collection that you were now selling. You wanted me to keep some of the fruits while at the same time, in contradiction to such generosity, you accused me of treachery, of being a petty opportunist. Laure herself confirmed all this to me when I ran into her one evening at Robert de Balkany's, who also defended me. I learned from Laure that you were telling everyone that I had received commissions on all her purchases. Even if I had, there wouldn't have been anything irregular about that, but it was an enormous lie. A dealer once offered me a percentage but I replied that the sum in question would be deducted from the selling price he was asking you. I made Laure laugh by adding that if I had received such generous commissions, I would have immediately bought a château where I would have been delighted to receive her.

Another subject that undoubtedly made you jealous and angry was the half-page article about me in Le Figaro *at the time of the sale. A journalist had called me to request an interview about your collections. I told her that I was not a good subject and that she should talk to you. She insisted, conducted the interview skillfully, and the article was published. Everyone congratulated me, but not a word from you. Valérie Duponchelle titled her article "Patrick Hourcade ou l'éloge de l'ombre" [Patrick Hourcade or Praise for the Shadow]. She mainly wrote about me and a little about you. You smiled to my face but behind my back the knives were out.*

All this was despicable, lamentable, and, for me, painful, which was probably what you wanted, as furious as you were to see me leave. Gianni Versace invited Franck and me to his house on Lake Como. He wanted me to come to Miami the following summer. He was killed there, a week before my planned departure.

My poor Karl,

You were gaining weight, you couldn't hide it, and it earned you the nickname Bibendum [Michelin Man]. But there was a good reason for that unfortunate state: you were depressed, and you knew perfectly well how to hide that from others. But what you hid from yourself was what you had loved, going so far as to claim before a compliant audience that you had only lived at Grand-Champ a very short time and had never loved it. Once again you were denying yourself, willingly confining yourself to the cherished prison of your convictions, which you no doubt would have shared later in improbable memoirs. But you cannot rewrite the past as you please, especially if you have lived it differently.

So, I ask you to forgive me, dear Karl. I was irritated with you at the time and failed to grasp the depth of your despair.

THE FIRST CANCER

You hid it well from all of us.

Why did you tell me that we were lucky? Why did you write to me that you would never be happy?

You were obviously suffering, but always guarded and proud, you didn't want to talk about it. You missed Jacques, you missed your mother, I was leaving and you were letting me go, you even encouraged me, I can see that now. You did not want me to know of your distress. Many of your friends had either been rejected or were dead...

"To lose one's friends is to lose a part of oneself."

— RAYMOND ARON

Money, you had to earn it; fashion, photography were your daily drugs to make you feel triumphant and forget your misfortunes. You became the idol of this falsely ideal, supposedly marvelous world. Surrounded, adulated, adored, you were alone with your destiny: apparently so happy, but deep inside, overwhelmed by grief and bankruptcy. Cancer is a scourge that is anything but painless. This first cancer, no one saw it, no one suspected it. After giving you the bad news that you would need to undergo a difficult operation to remove the tumor, the doctor was surprised by your reply, "You can go now, that is of no use to me." He had never heard such words from anyone he had treated before. The following years were very difficult for you, but you resisted and eventually recovered. Your success was phenomenal. Your great self-control, your draconian regime, the new body that you brought into being marked the beginning of a long decade. The family and friends who had disappeared were replaced with a universe of work, the promise of eternal youth, the exciting atmosphere of the studio, the vibrant lights of the catwalk, the nights and days that followed upon one another without cease, surrounded by all those people who helped you, worked with you, for you, for the success of the image, your image. They loved you as sincerely as you loved them, but in the end they all returned to their own homes, leaving you alone.

⁎

LAGERFELD AND VOLTAIRE

"A repeated lie becomes the truth," Karl used to say. Voltaire must have liked to believe it too, he who invented invented illegitimate origins from high nobility…

"My mother was first cousin twice removed from the Kaiser. My father was a Swedish baron." Karl also told Bernard Pivot, "My mother was the daughter of a high Prussian magistrate. My father, governor of Westphalia under the Emperor William II." And on like that happily!

All this was swept away with the click of a mouse by Wikipedia and by Alicia Drake's book *The Beautiful Fall* a few years later. Your mother's maiden name was Bahlmann, a lingerie saleswoman before she married Otto. No, Dad, a good bourgeois German, did not invent powdered milk, which had been created a century earlier by an American. But the important thing was to believe in it like Voltaire, and thus to behave with nobility and elegance. Both of you, for that matter, were attracted to people of power. Voltaire collected affinities with kings and queens; Karl never found fault with the upper crust and liked to suggest a proximity to the grand magnates of Capitalism.

Other traits the two shared were a sense of humor and love of repartee, earning them immediate success and a captivated audience. And also: constant concern for people, for others. Voltaire took in several hundred watchmakers to produce in Ferney that which they could no longer freely produce in Geneva, while Karl, without saying a word, restored at his own expense the dilapidated dwelling of David, the custodian of Hôtel Pozzo.

I do not know if Voltaire, like Karl, who did it naturally, devoted himself to people without watching the time, from the humblest to the most important. Karl's late arrivals were the result of his generosity with his time, which he gave to everyone.

But to avoid going overboard in our comparison, in addition to the differences in the respective creations of these two characters, and in their fame, we must note that Voltaire was a brilliant businessman, and that Karl, unfortunately, was not.

⁂

FREEDOM

"To be free is to accomplish a work that resembles us."

— HENRI BERGSON

You always helped me in all my choices. When I discovered a passion for ice skating and wanted to support the sport, you encouraged me. But after our breakup, a completely new destiny opened for me, a career I could not possibly have pursued if I had stayed with you.

On the evening of the opening of my first photography exhibition, at the Chapelle Saint-Louis de la Salpêtrière in Paris, I see ancient Pythia coming toward me in the dim light, her silver hair a halo around her enigmatic face. Dominique Issermann, master of black and white, a photographer from the glory years of Vogue. *I watched her approach, eyes fixed on me. She said, "You know what? You are free!" I kissed her to thank her for her words, which were so appropriate. She had understood everything.*

The freedom to express myself as suits me, with the techniques I choose, topics not imposed by anyone else: I found it in the end. And I realized how far I had come since I read your last letter that morning. I read it again later and saw that you were setting me free, yes, that's probably what you wanted, too. Without it I would never have stepped forward the way I did at the Saltpêtrière, and then again at Réfectoire des Cordeliers in Paris. My career after Vogue *and* Égoïste *allowed me to express myself completely. I also explored video, design, and now monumental sculpture. We designed some exhibitions together. I remember the Museo d'Arte Moderna of Rome with the* Percorso di Lavoro, *the story of your work for the Fendi sisters. Since then, Versailles and the Pushkin Museum have allowed me to renew the art of highlighting the work of others. I love my life, and I owe it to you, too.*

No doubt you wanted me to follow this new destiny, and that left you a little more alone.

⌘

BRIEF ENCOUNTERS

A century had ended and another was beginning; our paths, you in fashion and me in the world of art, had definitively diverged. But life always has its surprises.

Franck had decided to go to a small bookstore in Faubourg Saint-Honoré to discover a very intimate exhibition on Boutet de Monvel, an early twentieth-century artist with a very neat and bourgeois style. You certainly were familiar with the artist in question and appreciated his work.

What had to happen, happened: we had only been there a matter of minutes when the door opened and there you were standing before me. After our initial surprise, our manners took over. Franck was talking to the bookseller. You said you had some time and settled into a comfy chair, ready to hold court. Outside I saw your foot soldiers trying to get the details of the theater of our meeting. Meanwhile, Franck's occasional friend Martin, a German lawyer, struck up a conversation with you in German. He had a great deal of admiration for you and was peppering you with questions. You tended to respond in monosyllables; you were not very happy and Martin did most of the talking. Franck was doing his shopping, delighted with the embarrassing situation. You stayed there in your chair and I ended up talking to you about a painting we had on the wall at Le Mée by the artist on exhibit, very Gazette du Bon Ton. *You said loudly that it was much more beautiful than anything on display there. So I changed the subject and told you about an interesting lot of expressionist graphics in an upcoming sale. You replied, offhand, that you already knew about it, but obviously you didn't. But I knew you would look into it. Culture was our glue.*

One evening, Patrick Mauboussin, who had been my partner in discovering aviation design, invited me out to the newest fashionable restaurant, Matis on the Champs-Élysées. It was a night spot; velvet and candles created an intimate space where socialites came to gossip about those who were not there. The owner was a celebrity of old Parisian nightlife, pre-AIDS. We were waiting for our desserts to arrive when I saw you standing opposite me. You were clearly as surprised as I was. I was happy to see you, but it was your expression that brought a smile. Beaming and waving, you said in the sweetest voice, "Oh! Patrick! How are things?" Without waiting for an answer you sat down a few feet away. Two men were with you, certainly

Sébastien Jondeau and another boy I didn't bother trying to identify. Our dessert arrived. I looked at you a moment in profile. You were very focused, as usual, on a conversation with yourself, but you had slid a hand onto your neighbor's shoulder, a gesture of familiarity that was new for you. Time had also passed, and I discovered the leather gloves and all the big metal rings on your fingers, which you used to complain were like sausages. That saddened me. Perhaps that gesture was meant to show how happy you were and in what good company, but I also imagined that the gloves were an accessory in the game of hide-and-seek with age, that dreadful taskmaster.

The manager of the place was Gérald, we had known each other a long time, and when I left, he rushed up to me to say, "You know, I gave Karl the name of my cardiologist, because he is having problems." Tongues in this place were always wagging, but Karl survived while poor Gérald died of a heart attack soon after.

⁂

THE LAST TIME

If I had occasion to think of you, it was usually when friends gave me your news; I was not particularly inclined to seek it. But there is a place that unites us by shared passion: Galignani, the lovely bookstore by the Tuileries, where we shared many fine moments discovering the most alluring books. Under the soft light coming in through the glass roof, the years seemed not to have touched the long shelves of varnished wood, nor the English furniture; it had not altered the warm, amber atmosphere bathing these works, the art books, novels, and biographies you so loved. I went there regularly, you quite often, so it was inevitable that sooner or later we would meet. One evening I had dropped by quickly to order a book. You were there, alone at the register near the door. You looked at me a bit embarrassed. I put my arms around you, kissed you, and said, "You are magnificent!" They would be my last words to you. I meant it sincerely but didn't have anything else to say. Your skin seemed hardened. You made as if to kiss me, still seeming embarrassed, but with a big smile. Then I turned and walked out without looking back. There was really nothing left for us to say to one another. It was the last time I saw you, a furtive gesture of intimacy in a place we loved.

Danielle, the fairy godmother of this palace of knowledge and discovery, invited me one day to present in her famous window one or two creations I had made for Pierre and his lovely Galerie du Passage. Loyal Bertrand, your regular agent, helped me on that. While I was away, you came by, examined the window and exclaimed, "But now it's Patrick's bookstore!" Another time, again for Pierre, I had invented lights for the stratospheric theme of the Big Bang, with softly colored planets. Seeing the photo, which did not convey depth, you declared, "So now Patrick is making lollipops with Pierre?"

⁂

THE TRIUMPH OF THE PUPPET

"It is time to bring the puppet home!" you said to your chauffeur one evening, your self-mockery evoking the extraordinary living, powdered, well-dressed image that you manipulated by invisible strings, moving it as you pleased before the crowd's enthusiastic gaze.

Every day, you proceeded with the methodical and detailed examination of your appearance. "Mirror, mirror on the wall..." Your ability to laugh at yourself kept you from narcissism, but you did not like the image that this mirror reflected back to you day after day, and knew perfectly well that time was not going to fix that. But drawing had taught you to correct the dreadful errors of the cruel passage of time. You did not like your mouth and so, for many years, you used a fan to screen it. Under your pencil, the mouth was erased, the fan then disappeared, and only the sunglasses and the ponytail were left, which slowly evolved into the perfect image of a Lagerfeld without defect.

> *"When you start with a portrait and seek pure form,*
> *a clear volume, through successive eliminations,*
> *you arrive inevitably at the egg."*
>
> — PABLO PICASSO

Your many drawings of this sanitized Karl became figurines, synthesized objects, simulacra of a person, idealized icons appealing, initially, to the world of fashion, and later to a broad audience, over the years spreading well beyond the boundaries of the world's cities. Your Karlovitch de Lagerfeld figurine became as famous as Andy Warhol's Campbell's Soup Cans. *The fashion world knew your tailleurs, the entire world knew your head.*

"We believe that we live only by our senses,
and that the world of appearances is enough for us. …
Beyond the surfaces, our gaze penetrates all the way to the soul."
— AUGUSTE RODIN

You always sought to hide yourself; your figurine was the ultimate makeup. Above all, you didn't want anyone trying to find out who the man behind the mask really was. But over time, you became more and more mechanical. From one interview to the next you said everything and its opposite, you mixed up quotes, but it didn't matter, the journalists never did any fact checking. What they liked were your sharp, incisive responses, your plays on words, and the stream of culture you produced for them. Once you were impassioned, now you had become automatized; you were freewheeling but had a very clear idea of yourself. At times we sensed a certain weariness, which you quickly swept under the carpet so as never to lose face.

⁎

PRE-CLOSING PANIC

"I cannot stand all these old guys who eye up the young ones. To me it smells like panic before closing time." You loved to say this every time the occasion allowed. It's a very common story, this nostalgia for a freshness long since faded, the vampire seeking youth when it passes within range. The image is comical but well founded, and I smile when I see that in due course you focused on putting these naked, athletic young bodies into your images, under the pretext of aesthetics. A flattering admirer, once asked, coyly, "But really, Karl, when you photograph these young people, don't you sometimes want to

put the camera down and get a closer look?" Cut to the quick, you answered, "Of course not! I am not like you!" Jacques would have liked to be your assistant on those shoots, no doubt.

You played the aesthete, but also satisfied your secret passions. You who hated to show yourself, here revealed an intimate side.

⁂

ANIMAL STORY

Choupette, a.k.a. "Guimauve du Blues Daphné."

One winter's day, a white cat penetrated your beloved solitude by way of a busy disciple, who was leaving on a trip. No, you didn't like Christmas, a family holiday, a childish and useless holiday. Solitude, you thought, suited you perfectly, and the animal was entrusted to your care for a few days only—it had not been abandoned. Many people were hovering around you at the time. Some, like the faithful Sébastien, knew how to give your daily life an almost family atmosphere. But this animal, one paw lightly resting on your notebooks, barely deigning you a glance, may have snubbed you at first. That's the secret of cats, especially a sacred Birman cat, before it came to rub its silk hair on the sleeve of your jacket, to mark you as its territory. That was all it took to give you new hope. You who had known very few pets, were immediately captivated by this new plaything.

> *"A familiar spirit haunts this sod*
> *and shall rule, judge, inspire*
> *All things in this empire;*
> *Perhaps a fairy, perhaps a god?"*
>
> — CHARLES BAUDELAIRE

The memory of an episode from your childhood that you shared with me—a small, charming, affectionate dog that ran to you one day and without warning died at your feet— sheds light on the distance you put between yourself and these faithful companions. Animals can be fragile, you discovered it that day, but you did not want to know. Laure's Jack Russell terrier, my husky with the one blue eye that you liked, and Dourak, Liliane's blond dachshund—there was no lack of animals around you. You had even, at my request, created the Lucy of Lammermoor costume for Laure's dog Lucy, named after the character in Sir Walter Scott's novel. It was all photographed for Vogue Paris *under the pretext of presenting jewelry. Laure, thrilled by the adventure, then offered you Ashton, whom you gave a home at Le Mée. Ashton was very ugly, but very comical, a failed Jack Russell as Laure described him. These little foxes with their tremendous reputations for leaping, for dynamism, with their indefatigable joie de vivre, veritable tonics, are the perfect image of your lively spirit, which hated animals and sleepy people. But this one, with his short, bowed legs, also had big ears raised like satellite antennas; there was nothing sophisticated about him. You were bewitched, you adored Ashton, who returned the affection fleetingly, occupied as he was with many other things than cuddling. He and the cat, arriving at the last minute, were the only ones you fawned over, you who detested "physical contact." Ashton died from too much running, without taking time to live. It brought back the bad memory of your childhood.*

Choupette was clearly the only one to uncover the feelings you refused to share, and since she was not expected to write her memoirs, you had nothing to hide from her. But the idea of using her as a marketing tool was as absurd as it was delusional. Lady Bardot wrote a letter to Choupette, hoping she would pass the message on to you that you should keep your hands off the other animals. Of course you didn't care. "If a woman wants to defend the minks, she only has to show them her hand, and she'll have one less finger," you said, laughing. Choupette was going to be a businesswoman, an heiress. That was quite offensive at the time of the Gilets Jaunes, whom you denigrated for their dirty clothing. But you only saw it as fun, as provocation, as successful marketing most of all. With Choupette, you could double the impact of the "puppet," and this winning duo made you very happy.

⌘

At my request, Karl dressed up Laure's dog for Vogue. *An unfortunate childhood incident with a dog had left him scarred, but he fussed over dogs in his country homes and they loved it. He similarly treated his cat like a little doll.*

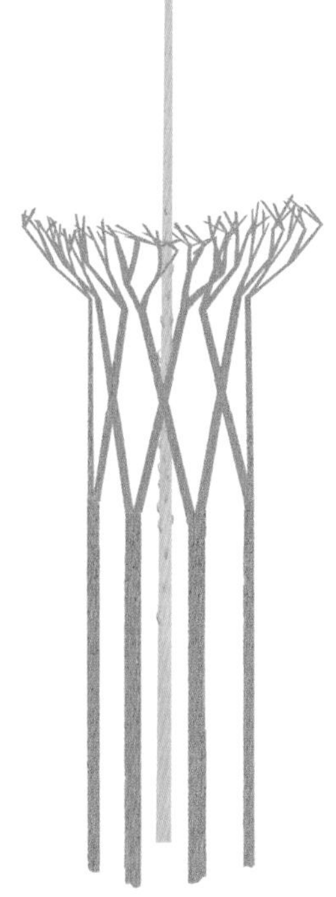

From Versailles to Vaux-le-Vicomte, from photography to design, sculpture, and installations, every day is a new day for me. I am a faithful adherent to this Lagerfeldian principle: keep your brain working.

Laure de Beauvau-Craon offered him this dog, which lived at Le Mée. Karl's assessment: "This dog is perfect: he is ugly and all he cares about is food, but he's quite amusing."

The cat was not his favorite animal. Choupette, an independent star, came into his life, and accompanied him until the end.

Like a color postcard from the bygone age of the belle Riviera, the last Rose Ball invitation designed by Karl.

THE AMBASSADRESS

"'Merit,' here is a word I detest, but in the case of Françoise Dumas, I am obliged to use it."

Of course you hated that word and repeated over and over again the reply of the Duke of Doudeauville, president of the Jockey Club. Upon hearing praise for the young Paul Bourget, who wanted to join, the duke replied, "Fortunately, there are still some among us who have no regard for merit!" But you have never been able to do without the extreme attention that Françoise has given you all these years. It was in Biarritz, the summer vacation spot that Françoise always loved, that you found her. She helped you on many events over the years and very quickly became indispensable to your fame and for your peace of mind. She was the faithful ambassadress for your hotly awaited media-fests, and you relied on her to handle all the dinners, ceremonies, and crucial meetings with government officials or influential and important people. She admired your ability to invent new table settings. And, along with Princess Caroline, she asked you to have a hand in the Rose Ball, a big Monaco event every spring. What did you not give of yourself to your beloved Principality of Monaco? You were the event's official artistic director. The first ball you organized was for the jubilee of Prince Rainier. You envisaged "Fifty Years of Images of Monaco" and summoned music stars and the year's top models.

Thirty years later, you were no longer there, but you were still able to provide the theme "The Riviera of the 1950s." To prepare the party, Françoise and the princess waited patiently at your place. You were late as usual but they were used to it. You finally arrived with a pile of books that you laid out on the table. You gave each of them a pair of scissors and showed them all of the illustrations that you thought were necessary for the project. Your hands were tired, you couldn't do it yourself, but your mind was sharp to the end as you planned your last dream ball.

When it opened, you were gone.

⌘

THE END

Tuesday, February 19, 2019

The night before, Luigi had a dream. A baby was sinking into a bottomless pit and someone was trying to save him. A hand desperately tried to grab the child as he receded from view, but he fell deeper and deeper. In Italy, this age-old dream signifies that a loved one will die. Luigi had worked for years at Chanel, but the company is huge and he had never crossed paths with Karl. The next day, he set off for work singing the famous song by Mina, "*Parole, Parole,*" which Karl had wanted for his last fashion show. A little while later, Luigi learned that Karl had died. He cried for two days.

Karl,

In a famous photo that Annie Leibovitz took at your house, your cat walking across the chaos of paper covering your work table, we don't know if it was carefully staged or the letting go of an old man caught up in his spells. You had always organized your disorder, but here everything was cast to the wind. Nights of work and solitude ended up filling what remained of life. Then the disease got worse and you had to abandon the table, never to come back, spending your last night in the hospital.

You wanted to live a hundred years. The ones you considered your enemies were dead, but you saw this as no reason to leave the world just yet. But the pernicious disease overtook you. You had tamed it once, but then it came back and was too much for you. I eventually learned of it and saw your efforts to maintain dignity to the end—your farewells on the screens at the end of the fashion shows, each more heroic than the last. You made your final exit at the Grand Palais, a venue you had put so much into so many times, with a final tribute to the spirit of Coco and the eighteenth century, inspired by Villa La Pausa. Locked into the straightjacket of fashion, girded with your false collars, camouflaged behind the dark glasses that masked your tired gaze upon the world, you played the "puppet" that society idolized. Sébastien was the last one, as you were dying, to meet the human eyes you hid from everyone else.

"I don't want to be buried, I don't want a ceremony." I don't want this, I don't want that... All your beautiful words up in smoke, like your body. My poor Karl, once dead, you had nothing more to say; for the first time in your

life, now over, you had lost your right to speak. Moreover, your repeated remarks to journalists, these so-called confidants, such as how the ashes of your mother, of Jacques, and your own should be united, are not likely to be carried out by those in charge. Because you had taken care to misplace the ashes of those you had loved, somewhere in the twenty-one thousand square feet of your storage room, cluttered and overflowing with your repressed memories, or perhaps in the house in Louveciennes, where they are unlikely to ever be found.

There was a small ceremony before closing the casket with your remains. The faithful and inconsolable Florentine was there before you, as you lay dressed like a star among his panoply of puppets. The day was dark, she was alone with you. She kissed you, probably the most affectionate message you received that day.

I received a very private invitation from Lady Marie-Louise to the ceremony on Mont-Valérien that I was not to share with anyone. Sébastien had also insisted that I come and I was touched that he had reached out to me. I was hoping, without really expecting it, that it would be a small, intimate affair. But after the white-gloved policeman had directed me where to park my car, I discovered a throng of people all dressed in black waiting at the top of the lane that led to the crematorium, a great shroud of grief blocking the road. I was seized by my usual fear of crowds and retreated behind the line of black limousines. I stood on a small sidewalk among the chauffeurs, who were absorbed in conversation about how to clean and shine their immaculate nickel-plated vehicles. There was a park behind us, bordered by a small ivy hedge. My hands clasped behind my back, as I calmly watched everything, I told myself that you were still keeping us waiting. When I felt a leaf slip between my fingers, I took it as a friendly botanical sign connecting us; ivy is a thread that connects the dead to the living. I plucked this small symbol and slipped it into my pocket.

I tried in vain to stay out of sight. I wanted to be one of the last into the back of the big hall, but the entrance was from the front, close to your coffin, which was as black as everything else. The crowd, seated, alert, stared at me as I walked in. Marie-Louise fortunately saved me from this awkwardness and guided me along another route. Then the ceremony that you did not want began. Lady Wintour was the first, speaking at length about your genius. It was then Princess Caroline's turn. Her voice was overcome by grief as she read a poem by Catherine Pozzi. It had been translated into German, your mother tongue, and here the sound of your friend's voice was more powerful than the meaning of the words. Years earlier, regarding your love for words, you had said to Pépita: "I can be moved by a poem I don't understand, what does it matter?" But you understood this poem well, about an impossible love taking flight after death.

Marie-Louise then read a note written by Jean-Jacques Aillagon, our famous former minister of culture, who had invited you to photograph Versailles. Lastly, Alain Wertheimer came up to the microphone and said these few words: "Karl was the kindest, most human person I have ever had the chance to meet." If you had heard them, they certainly would have pleased you. Then it was all over. I slipped out through the small garden bursting with white flowers, taking just the time to compliment Alain for his simple and sincere closing words.

Dear Karl,

Loved and "abandoned" by your father, your mother, and then Jacques, fleeing death that was constantly lurking, I will always see you as a heroic dinosaur condemned to its fate. The world adored you but you thought you would never be happy. You helped so many people, always to withdraw into your solitude. Your dark glasses did not conceal your kindness, but they hid your sadness. You wanted to live and go on living, you felt there was no world after you, but the world is still here, even without you.

⁎

AVE

Love of my life, my fear is I may die
Not knowing who you are or whence you came,
Within what world you lived, beneath what sky,
What age or times forged your identity,
Love beyond blame,

Love of my life, outstripping memory,
O fire without a hearth lighting my days,
At fate's command you wrote my history,
By night your glory showed itself to me,
My resting-place...

When all I seem to be falls in decay,
Divided infinitesimally
An infinite number of times, all I survey
Is lost, and the apparel of today
Is stripped from me,

Broken by life into a thousand shreds,
A thousand disconnected moments—swirl
Of ashes that the pitiless wind outspreads,
You will remake from what my spirit sheds
A single pearl.

Yes, from the shattered debris of my days,
You will remake a shape for me, remake a name,
A living unity transcending time and space,
Heart of my spirit, center of life's maze,
Love beyond blame.

— Catherine Pozzi (translated by Sebastian Hayes)

A RELIGIOUS MAN

Yes, you were baptized.

"I did not receive a religious education, for the simple reason that I was born Catholic in a Protestant country." A curious remark, especially when you added, "My parents suffered a great deal for their religion." Your mother, Elisabeth Lagerfeld, was the daughter of Karl Bahlmann, politician, member of Zentrum, the Catholic and moderate anti Fascist party, which played a leading role in the creation of the Weimar Republic. Some of its members would later join the resistance against the Nazis. Your father, Otto, was a member of the Old Catholic Church, Christians who did not want to hear talk of the pope and had a pronounced Jansenist tendency, values you always extolled. Your parents were not so much concerned with religion itself as with morality. While I never knew your father, I was able to see how much Elisabeth valued dignified behavior; it was a point of honor for her. Jacques's aimlessness and lack of discipline irritated her in the end. For their fierce pride and hard work, the Spanish couple who took care of her responded well to her ideal of human conduct. You, too, applied this discipline and dedicated every minute of your life to work. No, your mother was not an authoritative monster, but a woman who held true human values dear.

One day you proudly showed me three silver items made in Germany in the eighteenth century. They had been used at your baptism: two candlesticks and a ewer, which had contained, you said, holy water. A private sacrament, because you added that you were baptized at your parents' home. The objects were of fine craftsmanship, and you had always kept them with you, never sold them. But during the war, you were still a child and the religious had their hands full dealing with Nazi neo-paganism. Your parents, as much as they may have suffered a religious upbringing, certainly must have had other concerns regarding your education then.

There was never a cross in your house, but you were an admirer of Jansenism and Philippe de Champaigne. His admirable Saint Jerome in the Desert, *depicting an old man, praying alone and half naked before the cross in his grotto, was one of your favorite paintings and it was very hard for you to part with it. And the ascetic bedroom with its steel bed that you created in a house filled with riches and luxury was another sign of your attraction to contemplation. At first you wanted it gray, without decoration. You mentioned Port-Royal abbey and wanted a monk's cell with only a painting of Saint*

Elizabeth of Hungary by Mignard over your bed, in reference to your mother. Over time, more furniture arrived. You forgot about asceticism, you laughed, you talked about anything and everything. Religion did not interest you; you contemplated only the rational, fleeing the mystical. And true to yourself, you refused all ceremonies when you left this world.

I recently returned to Grand-Champ and had a memory of us walking past the small chapel at the entrance to the château. I was explaining its stylistic significance, with its choir screen decorated with the mystic lamb, and the opening in the roof behind the altar, similar to the back-lighting in the chancel of the church of Saint-Sulpice. You told me then that you wanted to restore it, and have it reconsecrated so you could put Jacques's ashes there and have Mass said for him and your mother. You would forget Grand-Champ and the little chapel, but you told Marie Ottavi, who had written so well about Jacques, that you wanted your ashes to be united with those of Jacques and Elisabeth. The duty of remembrance of the two people you had loved most in the world was your religion.

⁂

EPILOGUE

The fashion world, feeling the sense of loss and ennui of working without a dream after your departure, paid homage to you, declaring you "forever." Only humans can proclaim the dead forever. You, who loved fashion because it permanently erased the present, looking only to the future and never returning to the past, were declared "eternal." The irony would not have been lost on you.

Giant photos of you, again and again—and yes, that was really you—flooded the aquarium of the Grand Palais. We listened to Chopin, whom you never liked much, and watched crude tangos—that wasn't you—far from the soul of the Carlos Gardel you once mentioned. Women, and particularly actresses, were a vibrant presence. Lil Buk, a modern-day Marcel Marceau, brought poetry to this world of appearance, a lot of words, a flood of images praising your companionship and your life. Silvia Fendi, whom you've known since she was a little girl and became your Italian "accomplice," said with sorrow and humor that you were not dead, just late again. No, it was not you who was there but a crowd of mourners, famous people and celebrities, but also strangers and faces in the crowd who wanted to tell you how much they were going to miss you. And this world of fashion into which you had fled, over which you had ruled, could reappropriate Proust: "I don't miss anyone, except those I will never have to see again."

⁕

YOUR TESTAMENT

To Lucien, who, seeing time passing, regularly asked you to "make arrangements," you replied furiously, "You want me dead!"

It is quite probable that you jotted some names on paper, as you customarily did before getting into an airplane, a just-in-case list, crossing your fingers that it would be of no use. These people who accompanied you, some who helped you live, certainly deserve, in more ways than one, some sign of acknowledgment on your part. The matter of your multiple debts seems complicated and will take some time to sort out. It was your choice; "Après moi, le déluge," which Louis XV never said. But the law must run its course, and as I write this, nothing has been settled.

The houses will find new owners, but beyond these possessions to be sold off, what is left of all those objects you had discovered and loved? So I learned, again through Lucien, that you had your sights on a house in Louveciennes, a house "to go get some air," as you said. It was in this house that the Parnassian poet Leconte de Lisle lived and died, and he may likely have written the following verses there:

"One day, one hour, on the rough path pursued,
Under the burden of years bent,
Human spirit falters, fills with lassitude
And thinks back to days long spent."

— CHARLES-MARIE LECONTE DE LISLE

These verses may have inspired you, if you read them. And it is undoubtedly here that you arranged what had been the foundations of your culture and your taste, a discerning blend of prewar, trans-Rhine art and great French classical art. I am thinking particularly of this masterpiece by Dufresnoy, a painter close to Poussin, Rinaldo Abandoning Armida, *this dear Armida left behind who wanted to take revenge, all in all a story you knew well. This painting was your favorite. You wrote to me, "It represents for me (strangely) all the baroque music of Clorinda and Tancredi (another scene from* Jerusalem Liberated*)." Of course you were talking about the music of Monteverdi and probably meant to say "*Jerusalem Delivered.*" Nothing in the world would make you give up this painting, and in response to the museum that had requested it on loan, you wrote: "I adore my painting and I don't want to take it down for a second... They just have to show Poussin's drawing in the Louvre." You never wanted to part with it, and it is undoubtedly here that you hung it. But here, unfortunately, you may not have had much time to enjoy it; time passed too quickly.*

⁂

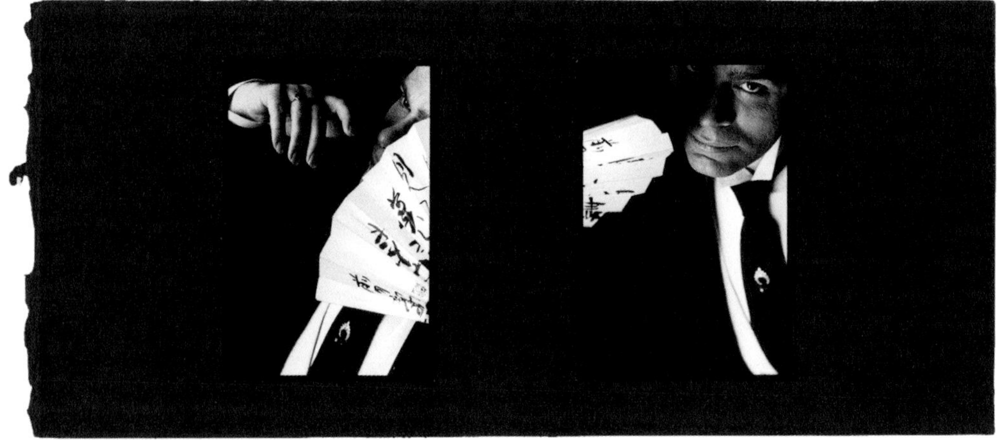

The fan hid your mouth, which you never liked, and you ended up discarding it, like all the rest.

And then, the day of his final leave-taking, this friend, with whom he spoke every day for the past forty years— the discreet Florentine Pabst, the most loyal of all—came to kiss him goodbye.

In all likelihood, it was in this house, in Bissenmoor, north of Hamburg, that Karl was baptized. But the photo with his parents, Elisabeth and Otto, may have been taken elsewhere. They loved him, and they probably also gave him his strong work ethic, as well as many other things, now faded memories.

Faire un meilleur
avenir avec les
éléments élargis
du passé.
J. W. v. Goethe

Karl Lagerfeld

There you have it, dear Karl, you are gone forever. Many will miss you, others less, but no one will be left indifferent. The motto here that you attribute to Goethe, "Build a better future by expanding on elements of the past," remains for all a most beautiful message of hope, a paean to life.

Yours,

Patrick

FELLOW TRAVELERS

Karl moved through many worlds and shared his life with many people. Some of them have found their way into this book:

THE CLOSEST:

Jacques de Bascher	Karl's only love †1989
Armelle de Bascher	Jacques's mother †2015
Diane de Beauvau-Craon	Jacques's fiancée
Laure de Beauvau-Craon	President of Sotheby's †2017
Françoise Dumas	Karl's trusted advisor
Caroline of Hanover	Princess of Monaco
Francine Crescent	Idol of *Vogue Paris* †2008
Lucien Frydlender	Karl's trusted business manager
Pierre Hebey	Lawyer, Karl's observer †2015
Geneviève Hebey	Karl's ideal woman
Sébastien Jondeau	Karl's assistant in his final years
Vern Lambert	Vintage fashion expert †1992
Florentine Pabst	Karl's oldest friendship
Anna Piaggi	Muse, *Vogue Italia* journalist †2012
Pierre Passebon	Eclectic gallerist, Karl's favorite
Liliane de Rothschild	Friend sharing passion for culture †2003
Élie de Rothschild	Baron and art collector †2007
Nicole Wisniack	Creator and director of *Égoïste*

IN THE REALM OF CULTURE:

Daniel Alcouffe	Chief Curator of Decorative Arts, Louvre
Marc Blondeau	Art advisor, critic, observer
Fabrice Bousteau	Director of *Beaux Arts Magazine*
Danielle Cillien-Sabatier	Director of Galignani bookstore
Franck Laigneau	Expert in vernacular art
Pierre Lemoine	Chief Curator, Versailles †2006
Bruno Pons	Historian of Faubourg Saint-Germain †1995
Bertrand Pizzin	Trusted advisor at Galignani
Alexandre Pradére	Historian, expert in antique furniture
Andrée Putman	Star of design †2013
Bertrand Du Vignaud	Heritage expert

IN THE REALM OF FASHION:

Gilles Dufour	He saw everything, from Chloé to Chanel
Marie-France Acquaviva	Pixie of early Chloé
Eva Campocasso	Whirlwind of early Chanel
Hervé Léger	More stylist than assistant †2017
Victoire de Castellane	Live wire at Chanel round two
Marie-Louise de Clermont-Tonnerre	The indispensable
Vincent Darré	The craziest, from Chloé to Fendi
Mathilde Favier	Child of fashion
Ines de la Fressange	Icon of French fashion
Sophie de Langlade	Her own woman, from *Vogue* to KL
Antonio Lopez	Illustrious illustrator †1987
Claudia Schiffer	Voluptuous icon, a touch of B.B.
Gianni Versace	Emperor of Italian fashion †1997
Virginie Viard	Trusted successor at Chanel
Éric Wright	Karl's most admiring assistant

NOT TO BE LEFT OUT:

Pierre Bergé	YSL, businessman, patron †2017
Fendi Family	Karl's beloved five Roman sisters
Yves Saint Laurent	Couturier of the century †2008
Alain Wertheimer	Chanel chief, Karl's faithful supporter

IN THE REALM OF PHOTOGRAPHY:

Caroline Lebar	Model, KL advertising director
Éric Pfrunder	Trusted assistant

A FEW JOURNALISTS:

Carlyne Cerf	Eccentric pixie, *Elle*, *Vogue*
Hebe Dorsey	Star of the *Herald Tribune* †1987
Pépita Dupont	*Paris Match* journalist and confidant
Suzy Menkes	*Herald Tribune* and *New York Times*
André Leon Talley	*Interview, WWD, MM, Vogue, W* and others
Anna Wintour	Condé Nast icon

The Vogue *years: Arthur Elgort plays paparazzo with Patrick in the Place du Palais Bourbon.*

ACKNOWLEDGMENTS

I would like to thank Alicia Drake, who had the courage to come to me while researching her book *The Beautiful Fall*, at a time when speaking about Karl was a risky affair. Her delicacy and tact allowed me to talk about him without fear.

I would like to thank Marie Ottavi, who preferred to focus on Jacques rather than publish a book on his more famous mentor. I am happy to have been able to help her write her honest book about the ill-fated hero, *Jacques de Bascher, dandy de l'ombre.*

I would particularly like to thank Raphaëlle Bacqué, who consulted me for her book *Kaiser Karl* and helped me recover memories that had dissipated somewhat over the years.

And my warmest thanks to Laurent Allen-Caron, who was the first to get me to work seriously on all the details of Karl's life, initially to produce Laurent Delahousse's television program "Un Jour, Un Destin" and later for his book *Le Mystère Lagerfeld.*

MY THANKS ALSO TO:
Pierre Passebon and Jacques Grange, for encouraging me to write this book; Hélène Guignard, who warmly welcomed me to her Château de Penhoët at Grand-Champ.

MY SINCERE GRATITUDE TO:
Barbara Baumel, Diane de Beauvau-Craon, Emmanuel Beffy, Professeur Paul Belaiche-Daninos, Eva Campocasso, Victoire de Castellane, Marie-Louise de Clermont-Tonnerre, Vincent Darré, Jean-René Delaye, Gilles Dufour, Françoise Dumas, Pépita Dupont, Mathilde Favier, Jérôme Gautier, Geneviève Hebey, Philippe Hourcade, Sébastien Jondeau, Alain Kraemer, Sophie de Langlade, Philippe Morillon, Florentine Pabst, Alexandre Pradère, Luigi Russo, Jean-Paul Scarpitta, Bertrand Du Vignaud.

PHOTOGRAPHIC CREDITS
t: top, b: bottom, c: center, l: left, r: right

Front cover: © Nicolas Kantor/Trunk Archive/PhotoSenso; pp. 6–7: © Herb Ritts/Trunk Archive/PhotoSenso; pp. 8–9: © All rights reserved; p. 13: © Karl Lagerfeld; pp. 14–15: © All rights reserved; p. 16 (collage): © Patrick Hourcade; p. 16t and l: © All rights reserved; p. 16c, bl and br: © Christie's Images Limited; p. 16r: © Patrick Hourcade; pp. 28–29: © SZ Photo/Max Scheler/Bridgeman Images; p. 30: © All rights reserved; p. 31: © Carol-Marc Lavrillier/Vogue Paris/The Condé Nast Publications Ltd; pp. 32–33: © The Guy Bourdin Estate, 2021/Reproduced by permission of Louise Alexander Gallery. All rights reserved; pp. 34–35: © Horst P. Horst/Vogue/The Condé Nast Publications Ltd; p. 36: © Philippe Heurtault; p. 37: © The Guy Bourdin Estate, 2021/Reproduced by permission of Louise Alexander Gallery. All rights reserved; p. 38: © Alfa Castaldi; p. 54: © Umberto Pizzi; p. 55: © Alexis Stroukoff; pp. 56–57: © The Guy Bourdin Estate, 2021/Reproduced by permission of Louise Alexander Gallery. All rights reserved; p. 58: © Philippe Heurtault; p. 59: © Patrick Siccoli/SIPA; p. 60: © Jack Nisberg/Roger-Viollet; p. 61: Horst P. Horst; pp. 62–63: © Jean-Claude Sauer/PARISMATCH/SCOOP; pp. 64–65: © Fotex/REX/Shutterstock; p. 66: © Christie's Images Limited; p. 67: All rights reserved; p. 68 (collage): © Patrick Hourcade; p. 68tl, tr and c: © Christie's Images Limited; p. 68cl: Getty Museum Collection; p. 68cr and b: © All rights reserved; p. 75: © Pierre Passebon Collection; pp. 76–77: © Patrick Hourcade; p. 77: © All rights reserved; p. 78: © Mary Russell; p. 83: © Jacques Schumacher; p. 84 (collage): © Patrick Hourcade; p. 84t: © Xavier de Bascher; p. 84c: © Alfa Castaldi; p. 86b: © Philippe Morillon; p. 99l: © Karl Lagerfeld; p. 99r: © All rights reserved; pp. 100–101: © The Guy Bourdin Estate, 2021/Reproduced by permission of Louise Alexander Gallery. All rights reserved; pp. 102–103: © Julien Danielo; pp. 104–105: © Patrick Hourcade; pp. 106–107: © Karl Lagerfeld; p. 108: © Patrick Hourcade; p. 109: © Karl Lagerfeld; p. 110: © Pierre Passebon; p. 119: © Mandoga Media/Alamy; pp. 120–21: © Alfa Castaldi; p. 122: © Serge Detalle; p. 123: © Françoise Labro; pp. 124–25: © Herbert Ohge; pp. 126–27: © Christie's Images Limited; p. 128 (collage): © Patrick Hourcade; p. 128t: Patrick Hourcade; p. 128l, c, r, and br: © Christie's Images Limited; p. 128bl: © All rights reserved: p. 134: © The Helmut Newton Estate/Maconochie Photography; p. 135 (collage): © Patrick Hourcade; p. 135tl: © Vladimir Sichov; p. 135tr: © Oskar Schlemmer/Art Collection 2/Alamy; p. 135bl: © Pierre Vauthey/Sygma/Getty Images; p. 135br: © APF Lewandowki-Beylard; p. 136: © Mark Kauffman/LIFE/Getty Images; p. 137: © Karl Lagerfeld; p. 138: © Max Scheler Estate/Focus/Cosmo; p. 139: © Karl Lagerfeld; p. 140 (collage): © Patrick Hourcade; p. 140 (photographs): All rights reserved; p. 160: © Gamma/Keystone/Getty Images; p. 161t: © Alain Benainous/Getty Images; p. 161b: © Christie's Image Limited; pp. 162–63: © Stephane Cardinale/Corbis/Getty Images; pp. 164–65: © Manuel Litran/PARISMATCH/SCOOP; p. 166: © All rights reserved; pp. 176–77: © Max Scheler/Max Scheler Estate/Agentur Focus; pp. 178–79: © Patrick Hourcade; p. 179: © Alfa Castaldi; p. 180: © Patrick Hourcade; p. 184 (collage): © Patrick Hourcade; p. 184 (photograph): © Jean-Luce Huré; p. 199: © Daniel Jouanneau; p. 200: © Patrick Hourcade; p. 201: © Bruno Lépolard; p. 202: © All rights reserved; p. 203: © akg-images/picture alliance; p. 204: © PLS Pool/Getty Images; p. 214: © David Seidner; p. 215 (collage): © Patrick Hourcade; p. 215c: © Abaca Press; p. 215bl: © All rights reserved; pp. 216–17: © All rights reserved; p. 219: © Patrick Swirc/modds; p. 222: © Arthur Elgort.

Every effort has been made to identify photographers and copyright holders of the images reproduced in this book. Any errors or omissions referred to the Publisher will be corrected in subsequent printings.

EXECUTIVE EDITOR
Suzanne Tise-Isoré
Style & Design Collection

EDITORIAL COORDINATION
Lara Lo Calzo

GRAPHIC DESIGN
Lucrezia Russo

TRANSLATION FROM THE FRENCH
Robert Burns/Language Consulting Congressi, Milan

COPY EDITING AND PROOFREADING
Lindsay Porter

PRODUCTION
Élodie Conjat

COLOR SEPARATION
Atelier Frédéric Claudel, Paris

Printed in Portugal by Printer Portuguesa

Simultaneously published in French as
Karl, une si longue complicité

Flammarion S.A.
87, quai Panhard-et-Levassor
75647 Paris cedex 13
editions.flammarion.com
styleetdesign-flammarion.com

20 21 22 3 2 1
ISBN: 978-2-08-024371-3
Legal Deposit: 10/2021